New Directions for
Child and Adolescent
Development

Reed W. Larson
Lene Arnett Jensen
EDITORS-IN-CHIEF

William Damon
FOUNDING EDITOR

Rethinking Positive Adolescent Female Sexual Development

Lisa M. Diamond
EDITOR

Number 112 • Summer 2006
Jossey-Bass
San Francisco

RETHINKING POSITIVE ADOLESCENT FEMALE SEXUAL DEVELOPMENT
Lisa M. Diamond (ed.)
New Directions for Child and Adolescent Development, no. 112
Reed W. Larson, Lenne Arnett Jensen, Editors-in-Chief

Microfilm copies of issues and articles are available in 16mm and 35mm, as well as microfiche in 105mm, through University Microfilms, Inc., 300 North Zeeb Road, Ann Arbor, Michigan 48106-1346.

ISSN 1520-3247   electronic ISSN 1534-8687

NEW DIRECTIONS FOR CHILD AND ADOLESCENT DEVELOPMENT is part of The Jossey-Bass Education Series and is published quarterly by Wiley Subscription Services, Inc., a Wiley company, at Jossey-Bass, 989 Market Street, San Francisco, California 94103-1741. Periodicals postage paid at San Francisco, California, and at additional mailing offices. Postmaster: Send address changes to New Directions for Child and Adolescent Development, Jossey-Bass, 989 Market Street, San Francisco, CA 94103-1741.

New Directions for Child and Adolescent Development is indexed in PsycInfo, Biosciences Information Service, Current Index to Journals in Education (ERIC), Psychological Abstracts, and Sociological Abstracts.

SUBSCRIPTIONS cost $90.00 for individuals and $220.00 for institutions, agencies, and libraries.

EDITORIAL CORRESPONDENCE should be e-mailed to the editors-in-chief: Reed W. Larson (larsonr@uiuc.edu) and Lene Arnett Jensen (jensenl@cua.edu).

Jossey-Bass Web address: www.josseybass.com

CONTENTS

1

This chapter introduces and defines the notion of positive adolescent female sexuality and summarizes the diverse perspectives that each of the chapters in this volume takes regarding this topic.

Introduction: In Search of Good Sexual-Developmental Pathways for Adolescent Girls

Lisa M. Diamond

Historically, research has portrayed adolescent sexuality as a source of problems and risks rather than an integral aspect of human development. This is particularly true with regard to research on adolescent girls, traditionally cast as sexual gatekeepers whose primary task is to fend off boys' sexual overtures and set aside their own sexual desires in order to reduce their risks for pregnancy and sexually transmitted diseases. Michelle Fine powerfully identified and critiqued this cultural framework over fifteen years ago in a seminal review article on school-based sex education discourses (Fine, 1988). By spotlighting the multiple ways in which sociocultural forces function to silence girls' sexual voices and stunt their sexual agency, Fine's analysis provided an important spark for researchers to begin creatively reimagining what healthy, self-affirming sexuality might look like for girls and how we might best identify and promote it.

In the ensuing years, an increasing number of thoughtful and constructive critiques have challenged negatively oriented perspectives on sexual risk. These critiques have argued for more sensitive, in-depth, multimethod investigations into positive meanings and experiences of adolescent female sexuality that will allow us to conceptualize (and, ideally, advocate for) healthy sexual-developmental trajectories. This volume takes up the challenge by presenting a series of chapters by accomplished sexuality researchers setting forth diverse perspectives on healthy sexuality development among adolescent girls.

NEW DIRECTIONS FOR CHILD AND ADOLESCENT DEVELOPMENT, no. 112, Summer 2006 © Wiley Periodicals, Inc.
Published online in Wiley InterScience (www.interscience.wiley.com) • DOI: 10.1002/cd.158

These perspectives emphasize the complex interactions among ideological, biological, cultural, familial, intrapsychic, and interpersonal influences, and they underscore the importance of using multiple methods to investigate sexual ideation and experience.

First, certain clarifications are in order. Just what is meant by "positive sexuality" or "healthy sexual development"? These terms might seem relatively straightforward, but a review of current social scientific articles reveals a broad range of (typically implicit) definitions. The authors in this volume generally hew to the interpretations offered by the World Health Organization (2004), which convened a meeting on sexual health in 2002 to clarify such definitions. According to WHO, sexuality "is a central aspect of being human" that incorporates eroticism, intimacy, pleasure, reproduction, and one's own gender identity. Manifestations of sexuality include not only sexual behaviors, but wishes, desires, fantasies, attitudes, roles, and relationships. WHO also views sexuality as inherently multidimensional, integrating biological, cultural, social, economic, psychological, ethical, and spiritual factors. "Positive" or "healthy" sexuality, then, requires that individuals have adequate freedom and knowledge to pursue safe and satisfying sexuality. In the compelling words of the WHO, "Sexual health is a state of physical, emotional, mental and social well-being in relation to sexuality; it is not merely the absence of disease, dysfunction or infirmity. Sexual health requires a positive and respectful approach to sexuality and sexual relationships, as well as the possibility of having pleasurable and safe sexual experiences, free of coercion, discrimination and violence" (2004, p. 3).

The chapters in this volume provide diverse and fascinating perspectives on this important goal. We begin with Carolyn Tucker Halpern's integrative synthesis of biological contributions to positive female sexual development and their interactions with social and interpersonal factors. In her developmental systems approach, set out in Chapter Two, biological factors (specifically, hormones) are shown to have probabilistic rather than deterministic effects on sexual experience and behavior, which must always be considered in the light of their social and cultural contexts. Furthermore, she calls for attention to a broader range of potential hormonal contributions to adolescent female sexuality than has previously been considered. For example, she highlights the potentially important role of oxytocin, a neuropeptide hormone that has been shown in animal research to be related to attachment and affiliative processes. Given that such processes are clearly relevant to women's experiences of sexual desire and attraction, she calls for greater developmental research on their role in normative female sexual development. Such approaches offer exciting new directions for integrative biosocial investigations of positive sexual development.

Julia Graber and Lisa Sontag offer another powerful example of this integrative approach in their review of the psychological and social impacts of puberty on girls' self-concepts, particularly regarding sexuality. They demonstrate in Chapter Three how the hormonal and social transformations of puberty affect not only girls' bodies and brains, but also their feelings about themselves, perceptions of their bodies, and engagement in their social world. They focus particular attention on girls' body images and how pubertal changes interact with concurrent peer influences to shape adjustment. Importantly, these changes are shown to have differential influences on girls as a function of diversity in maturational timing. Their analysis prompts us to consider a multifaceted conceptualization of "positive" puberty that takes a broad range of interacting processes into account.

Moving into the realm of family relationships, Eva Lefkowitz and Tara Stoppa provide in Chapter Four a unique, positive perspective on parent-adolescent communication about sexuality. Contrary to most prior research on this topic, which has typically emphasized the specific messages that parents communicate about avoiding pregnancy and sexually transmitted diseases, Lefkowitz and Stoppa focus on the process of communication rather than simply its content. Their approach elucidates how parents subtly and not so subtly shape girls' sexual-emotional trajectories through implicit and explicit discussions of sexual values and attitudes. By examining not just what parents say but how different types of messages are transmitted in the context of an unfolding interpersonal interaction, they reveal communication dynamics that help us to understand the antecedents of potentially positive sexual-developmental trajectories.

Chapter Five, by L. Monique Ward, Kyla Day, and Marina Epstein, focuses on the potentially positive roles for the media in adolescent girls' sexual development. Contrary to prevailing views of media influences as uniformly negative, stereotypical, and hypersexualized, they emphasize the positive contributions that media images and messages can make to girls' development. Not only can certain types of media outlets provide sexual information that may be missing elsewhere, but some media outlets offer diverse sexual role models for girls that might allow them to observe and vicariously experience romantic and sexual scripts in a safe context. This analysis highlights the fact that many young women's use of media is proactive rather than reactive, involving the active selection of media content (some of it proudly antimainstream, such as zines) that they find compelling, appealing, and informative. Ward, Day, and Epstein demonstrate the importance of combining critiques of negative media influences with a focus on the potentially positive functions of media images that might help girls to find creative models of sexual self-expression and empowerment.

Finally, Deborah Tolman, one of the most active advocates for more positive approaches to adolescent female sexual development, provides a powerful set of reflections on what nonetheless remains missing from such approaches: a critical focus on compulsory heterosexuality, Adrienne Rich's (1980) conceptualization of the hegemonic cultural privileging of patriarchal heterosexual relations. In a tour de force that weds feminist theory with insights into social scientific methodology, Tolman points the way toward new strategies of asking complementary questions about girls' and boys' sexual feelings and experiences that make more visible the broader cultural nexus of race, class, and gender in which sexual development unfolds.

What Sets Positive Approaches Apart?

To provide a context for these authors' insights and findings, it is useful to step back and consider the process of conducting positively oriented research on adolescent female sexuality. What makes this process and its findings different from traditional approaches? If the programs of research spotlighted in this volume represent exemplars of such an approach, what unites them, given the notable diversity of their topics, theories, and methods?

It is certainly not a narrow focus on "good" aspects of sex or a denial of the challenges and risks that face female youths. Rather, many of the chapters explicitly address potential negative sexual-developmental outcomes such as pregnancy and sexually transmitted diseases. Yet the context in which such negative phenomena are considered is notably different than it is in traditional research on adolescent sexuality. This is because the positively oriented approaches represented in this volume are distinguished in a number of ways.

Interplay Among Contextual Factors. Contrary to research approaches that treat sexual behavior as if it occurs in a vacuum, all of these chapters place considerable emphasis on the multiple interacting contexts in which sexual development occurs: peers, parents, romantic relationships, and a media-saturated, patriarchal, heterosexist culture. Importantly, none of these contextual factors operates in isolation; rather, they intersect to push and pull girls' sexual development in different ways at different developmental stages. Hence, efforts to promote positive sexual-developmental trajectories among girls will be compromised unless such contexts are taken into account. No matter what we might do to bolster a girl's psychosocial adjustment, interpersonal skills, emotion regulation, sexual knowledge, and self-efficacy, we must contend with the fact that her larger social environment can work either for or against such efforts. For example, Graber and Sontag point out that girls with a higher body mass index were less likely to date, suggesting that they were not considered attractive dating partners by the boys in their social networks. Thus, even if we succeed in communicating acceptance of a more diverse range of positive body types among girls, this may have little impact if their peers, parents, and the media continue to relentlessly communicate a restrictive, excessively thin ideal. Thus, promotion of positive sexual-developmental trajectories for girls necessarily involves the promotion of positive cultural change across a range of interconnected contexts. Ward, Day, and Epstein's final "wish list" of positive media changes is an excellent example of thinking through to what sorts of environments might be necessary to optimize girls' positive sexual development. Tolman's call to action is more radical, advocating a systematic dismantling of the ideology of compulsory heterosexuality that continues to constrain notions of "normal" sexuality among both girls and boys.

NEW DIRECTIONS FOR CHILD AND ADOLESCENT DEVELOPMENT • DOI: 10.1002/cad

Integration of Biological and Social Factors. Historically, research on sexuality has tended to be segregated between approaches that focus on cultural factors and approaches that focus on biology. As Tolman and Diamond have argued previously (2001), this has long hampered investigations into women's sexuality and is particularly detrimental for understanding sexual development, given the notable biological transitions that characterize the adolescent years. Yet biology is obviously not destiny, and thus the most effective approaches are sensitive to the complex, nuanced interactions between biological processes and their psychological, social, and cultural contexts. These chapters exemplify such an approach.

Attention to Processes Outside the Strictly Sexual Domain. Sexual feelings and behaviors are obviously nested within broader psychological, cognitive, and interpersonal processes. Thus, attempts to understand and promote positive female sexual development must understand how factors such as social competence, emotion regulation, self-esteem, body image, and communication skills (to name just a few) influence how girls experience, understand, manage, and act on sexual desires. Each chapter in this volume views sexual development as nested within these concurrent processes and domains, providing a richer and more multifaceted understanding of the processes that both promote and hinder positive sexual development.

Life Course Perspective. A recurring theme throughout the chapters is that positive sexual development cannot simply be turned on at sexual maturation. Rather, positive sexual-developmental trajectories have their origins much earlier, in pathways of positive interpersonal and psychosocial development that become established in childhood. The transitions of sexual maturation weave together different strands of psychological, physical, and social development in powerful and potentially transformative ways. Unless those individual strands already contain the foundations for healthy self-concepts, feelings of agency, and social competence, it is unlikely that girls can suddenly repair prior deficits and craft new and healthy sexual pathways to adulthood. Thus, advocacy for positive sexual development must begin with advocacy for positive child psychosocial development more generally.

Emphasis on Relationships. Research has conclusively demonstrated that one of the most distinctive aspects of female sexuality—not only during adolescence but throughout the life course—is its sensitivity to relational contexts. For girls, experiences of sexual desire, sexual agency, and sexual self-concept are often directly linked to their experiences of satisfaction, confidence, and mutual intimacy with their romantic or sexual partner. Thus, understanding this relational component of girls' sexuality, and helping girls to master specifically relational skills, is fundamental to understanding and promoting positive female sexual development. At the same time, critical ambivalence about the relational aspects of female adolescent sexuality is warranted, as it has its roots in historical and ideological constructions of female sexuality as acceptable only within the confines of committed (ideally marital, but always heterosexual) relationships. Thus, as

Tolman's chapter emphasizes, we must remain deeply critical of the pervasive forces in girls' environments that reinforce such potentially negative, patriarchal, and heterosexist messages. The goal should be to investigate and understand not only relational influences on sexuality but also how girls can develop a strong and positive individual sense of ownership over their sexual feelings.

Looking to the Future

With this diverse and powerful group of analyses as a road map, what might we expect and demand from future research on positive female sexual development? Certainly, one pressing need is more systematic attention to issues of sexual desire and pleasure among female adolescents. Tolman's work (1991, 2002) has long highlighted the "dilemmas of desire" that confront girls growing up in a culture that continues to cast female sexuality as inherently dangerous. We must provide girls with the space and support to develop positive, empowering sexual self-concepts that include desire and pleasure. It is ironic that although the broader culture (and, of course, pharmaceutical companies) has drawn increased attention to low sexual desire among adult women as a form of sexual "dysfunction," the potential roots of this dysfunction in the negative messages we send to adolescent girls about the dangers of sexual desire and pleasure remain underinvestigated. Clearly, we require a more thorough understanding of—and advocacy for—healthy trajectories of erotic desire in order to truly foster girls' sexual self-concepts and empower them to make positive sexual choices.

Greater attention to same-sex desire, affection, and behavior is also important. Clearly there has been a laudable surge in research on lesbian, gay, bisexual, and transgendered youth over the past twenty years that has highlighted how the cultural privileging of heterosexuality can create developmental challenges for youths whose desires fall outside this normative ideal. Yet we must guard against a strict bifurcation of the adolescent population into "gay" and "straight" youths, with correspondingly distinct developmental trajectories. Rather, research increasingly suggests that many heterosexual youths have (sometimes highly significant) same-sex romantic and sexual desires and experiences, just as many gay and lesbian youths have (sometimes highly significant) other-sex romantic and sexual desires and experiences (Diamond, 2003a, 2003b, 2005). Thus, the most comprehensive and generative models of positive adolescent sexual development must include both same-sex and other-sex sexuality among both heterosexual and sexual-minority youths.

Finally, we require more integrative investigations into the necessary intersections between positive trajectories of female and male development. Although this volume focuses specifically on female adolescents and emphasizes the importance of gender-specific models, we must remain mindful of the fact that cultural constructions of womanhood go hand in hand with constructions of manhood. Thus, positively oriented, forward-thinking approaches to sexual development will be most effective when they take these interbraided cultural constructions into account. As Tolman explicitly argues, cultural messages and contexts facing girls are accompanied by complementary messages and contexts facing boys, and it is by internalizing ideologies of both femininity and masculinity that girls and boys enact and reproduce patriarchal dynamics. Thus, although it will remain helpful and important to investigate trajectories of positive sexual development separately for boys and girls, we must also work to develop systematic, integrative models of their necessary interrelationship.

My hope is that in another fifteen years, the field of developmental psychology will have generated multiple, nuanced perspectives on positive sexual development that model increasingly complex interactions among biological, cultural, intrapsychic, and interpersonal influences and account for broad cultural ideologies as well as microlevel interpersonal dynamics. Correspondingly, in another fifteen years, girls and boys may be growing up with expanded conceptualizations of sexuality that emphasize autonomy, agency, and knowledge and represent the full range of their diverse desires and experiences. The powerful chapters in this volume represent an important step toward this goal.

References

Diamond, L. M. (2003a). Was it a phase? Young women's relinquishment of lesbian/bisexual identities over a five-year period. *Journal of Personality and Social Psychology, 84,* 352–364.

Diamond, L. M. (2003b). What does sexual orientation orient? A biobehavioral model distinguishing romantic love and sexual desire. *Psychological Review, 110,* 173–192.

Diamond, L. M. (2005). What we got wrong about sexual identity development: Unexpected findings from a longitudinal study of young women. In A. Omoto & H. Kurtzman (Eds.), *Sexual orientation and mental health: Examining identity and development in lesbian, gay, and bisexual people* (pp. 73–94). Washington, DC: American Psychological Association Press.

Fine, M. (1988). Sexuality, schooling, and adolescent females: The missing discourse of desire. *Harvard Educational Review, 58,* 29–53.

Rich, A. (1980). Compulsory heterosexuality and lesbian existence. *Signs, 5,* 631–660.

Tolman, D. L. (1991). Adolescent girls, women and sexuality: Discerning dilemmas of desire. *Women and Therapy, 11,* 55–69.

Tolman, D. L. (2002). *Dilemma of desire: Teenage girls and sexuality.* Cambridge, MA: Harvard University Press.

Tolman, D. L., & Diamond, L. M. (2001). Desegregating sexuality research: Combining cultural and biological perspectives on gender and desire. *Annual Review of Sex Research, 12,* 33–74.

World Health Organization. (2004). Sexual health: A new focus for WHO. *Progress in Reproductive Health Research, 67,* 1–8.

LISA M. DIAMOND *is associate professor of psychology and gender studies at the University of Utah.*

2

This chapter discusses biological contributions to adolescent female sexual development and, based on a developmental systems framework, suggests future research directions.

Integrating Hormones and Other Biological Factors into a Developmental Systems Model of Adolescent Female Sexuality

Carolyn Tucker Halpern

> Not even rats are hormone-driven automatons.
>
> Becker et al., 1992, p. 69

In a series of reports beginning in 1946, the World Health Organization (WHO; 1946, 1975, 1987) defined sexual health as "the integration of the somatic, emotional, intellectual, and social aspects of sexual being, in ways that are positively enriching and that enhance personality, communication, and love" (WHO, 1975, p. 41). More recently, the National Commission on Adolescent Sexual Health (Sexuality Information and Education Council of the United States, 1995) emphasized the applicability of this perspective to adolescence, noting that adolescent sexual health encompasses positive interpersonal relationships, emotional expression and intimacy, and personal body perceptions. Subsequently others (Ehrhardt, 1996; Satcher, 2001; Tolman, Striepe, & Harmon, 2003) have reiterated the point that sexual development is one of many facets of human development, and they have advocated for its study through an integrated lens that captures biology, behavior, and the cultural, social, and physical aspects of an adolescent's environment.

NEW DIRECTIONS FOR CHILD AND ADOLESCENT DEVELOPMENT, no. 112, Summer 2006   © Wiley Periodicals, Inc.
Published online in Wiley InterScience (www.interscience.wiley.com) • DOI: 10.1002/cd.159

Adopting this perspective, this chapter focuses on biological, particularly hormonal, contributions to adolescent female sexual development and situates their contributions to sexuality within a broader developmental science perspective. The chapter is divided into two sections. First, I briefly review information about sex hormones and review findings from illustrative empirical work, based on animals and humans, which has examined associations between sex hormones and aspects of female sexuality. In the second half, I suggest two directions for future research on adolescent female sexuality based on adoption of a developmental systems perspective.

Hormones and Their Contributions to Sexuality

Hormones are chemicals that are produced by endocrine cells and released into the circulatory system to be carried to target organs. There are two general classes, classified according to molecular structure: steroid and steroidlike hormones, derived from cholesterol and produced by the gonads, adrenal cortex, and thyroid (such as androgens and estrogens); and glycoprotein hormones and protein or peptide hormones such as oxytocin and vasopressin. The latter class of hormones acts through binding with receptors on the outer membrane of cells. Steroid hormones are lipid soluble, pass through the cell membrane, and bind to receptor proteins. The resulting complex binds to DNA. This binding action affects the synthesis of proteins, the foundation of biological processes.

Hormones can affect the action of other hormones and neurotransmitters, as well as the activity of glands and organs. Steroids can also regulate gene transcription (expression) and play a role in neuromaturation, affecting brain structure and function, which in turn affects behavior. In humans and other vertebrates, the hypothalamus controls the endocrine systems. Specialized neurons in the hypothalamus (neurosecretory cells) release neurohormones into blood vessels that carry them to other organs, such as the pituitary. One type of neurohormone is releasing factors (for example, gonadotropinreleasing hormone), which stimulate or inhibit the release of hormones by cells in the anterior pituitary. There are a variety of specialized hormones, such as growth hormone and luteinizing hormone, released by the pituitary (and special hypothalamic releasing factors controlling them). Pituitary hormones affect other endocrine glands and organs, including the adrenal gland and ovaries, to stimulate or inhibit their release of other hormones. Feedback mechanisms, positive and negative, from peripheral endocrine glands to the pituitary and hypothalamus regulate the system to maintain relatively constant hormone levels or regular cycles of varying hormone concentrations.

Hormonal action is pervasive. Hormonal activity, particularly that of androgens and estrogens, during the prenatal and pubertal developmental periods has been of particular interest in research on sexual differentiation and sexuality. Both males and females make steroid hormones, but in different amounts. In the prenatal period, hormones contribute to sexual differentiation (determining male versus female reproductive organs and genitalia) and sex differences in brain organization or structure. Hormonal prenatal effects have been categorized as organizational and are key to the biological definition of males and females. Before and during puberty, a resurgence of hormonal activity after a long period of relative quiescence starts a series of events that dramatically change physiology and physical appearance, ultimately leading to reproductive maturity. (For specifics of hormonally induced prenatal and pubertal change, see Becker, Breedlove, & Crews, 1992, and Brooks-Gunn & Reiter, 1990.)

Implicit linkages between hormones and sexuality are long-standing. Knowledge of basic elements of endocrinology (for example, the effects of castration on animal reproduction) has been evident since at least Aristotle (Bullough, 1994). More explicit associations between what were first labeled as hormones by Starling in 1905 and aspects of animal mating behavior were demonstrated in experiments conducted by researchers as early as the nineteenth century. The importance of pubertal increases in sex hormones to the heightened sexual interest apparent in human adolescents was long assumed in both lay and scientific thinking, but was not directly investigated until the early 1980s.

Animal Models. Because of controversy over human sexual research (see Bullough, 1994) and the capacity for experimentation, research with animals (rats in particular) has been used to apply behavioral endocrinology toward understanding human sexuality. Empirical evidence from animal models has been accumulating for decades (Boling & Blandau, 1939; Beach, 1976) and indicates that gonadal hormones play a significant role in sexual behavior. A variety of physiological mechanisms for hormonal effects have been demonstrated, such as binding to brain steroid receptors and modification of the sensitivity of sensory systems such as olfaction (Agmo, 1999). However, the extent to which animal work to date meaningfully informs us about various aspects of female sexual development is not always clear because of inexact animal analogues for human sexual constructs, such as desire, and questions about the ecological validity of indicators of female rat desire (for example, lordosis) even for rats.

In a wild environment, the female rat controls the pace of sexual interaction through a series of approach and running-away movements that puts the female into the "male's space" at certain points in the process and elicits the male's orientation response (McClintock & Adler, 1978). A subsequent runaway by the female activates pursuit by the male, typically followed by intromission. The typical observation area used in most past laboratory rat studies was small enough that the female was constantly in the male's space and thus did not have the control she would have had in a more natural setting. Some argue that "female [rat] sexual motivation has been almost totally ignored in laboratory studies" (Agmo, 1999, p. 144), as has female arousal, because of the absence of work on vaginal blood flow in female rats (Pfaus, 1996). These considerations underscore the need for caution in assuming consistent parallels between humans and other animals, and the developmental importance of context, even for rat sexuality.

Human Female Sexuality. Studies examining the effects of exogenous hormone administration to naturally and surgically postmenopausal women support the influence of estrogen therapy on various facets of sexuality, including desire and arousal (Sherwin & Gelfand, 1987; Sherwin, Gelfand, & Brender, 1985). The addition of testosterone improves these dimensions (Davis, 1998; Sherwin & Gelfand, 1987), and testosterone administration also enhances sexual motivation in the absence of estrogen administration (Bancroft, Sanders, Davidson, & Warner, 1983; Sherwin et al., 1985). However, evidence is not entirely consistent. Shifren et al. (2000), based on a sample of women who had undergone surgical menopause, found significant associations between testosterone administration and measures of sexual frequency and pleasure but, in contrast to Sherwin et al. (1985), not sexual desire or arousal, the sexual aspects that are theoretically most closely linked to hormonal input.

Results of studies examining sexual desire across the menstrual cycle phase are also mixed. Data do suggest increased sexual interest and desire, particularly if indexed by female initiation, in the menstrual follicular phase or at the time of ovulation, when estrogen and testosterone levels are increasing or at their peak (Adams, Gold, & Burt, 1978; Bancroft et al., 1983; Dennerstein et al., 1994; Harvey, 1987; Matteo & Rissman, 1984; Stanislaw & Rice, 1988). However, there is considerable individual variation (Bancroft, 2005; Meuwissen & Over, 1992). Studies tracking the simple occurrence of sexual activity suggests that external opportunity factors (contexts such as work schedules) are more influential than hormone levels (Palmer, Udry, & Morris, 1982). Psychological, affective, and contextual factors likely account for differences across studies (Bancroft, 2005).

Experimental and observational evidence linking hormones and sexuality in adolescent girls is even more mixed. Finkelstein et al. (1998) investigated the effects of exogenously administered estrogen and testosterone on the sexual interest and behavior of a clinical sample of ten- to nineteen-year-old hypogonadal adolescents. Significant effects of hormone administration were evident only for "necking" for girls; the theoretically important measure of sexual motivation was unaffected. Inconsistent findings also characterize observational studies. Udry, Talbert, and Morris (1986), in a cross-sectional study of a nonclinical sample of adolescent females, showed strong associations between sexual ideation, motivation, and testosterone. Hormone measures were not associated with sexual intercourse, which was interpreted as a function of stronger social sanctions against early female sexual activity. Linkages between pubertal changes in testosterone and coital transition were later demonstrated in a two-year longitudinal study of adolescent girls using similar measures (Halpern, Udry, & Suchindran, 1997). However, as in the Finkelstein et al. (1998) work, the important theoretical path between testosterone and sexual interest and motivation was not replicated in the longitudinal data (Halpern et al., 1997). Inconsistencies in associations between hormones and sexual motivation echo those seen in studies of adult women.

Other work has explored linkages between adrenal androgens and sexual attraction. For example, males and females from multiple age cohorts retrospectively report first becoming aware of sexual attraction at age ten; this reported age coincides with the approximate time, ages six to ten years, that the adrenal glands mature (Herdt & Boxer, 1993; Herdt & McClintock, 2000; McClintock & Herdt, 1996; Pattatuci & Hamer, 1995; Savin-Williams & Diamond, 2000). These findings are a better fit with theory, as attraction is conceptually linked to desire, but the retrospective nature of the data is problematic.

Many factors, both developmental and methodological, may contribute to discrepancies in hormonal associations with sexuality in investigations of adult and adolescent female sexuality. However, I suggest, as have others, that the key reason underlying empirical discrepancies and modestly sized associations is that increases in gonadal steroids are not sufficient "causes" of sexual desire or behavior. Rather, hormones, and any other biological or psychosocial factor, contribute to sexual development in a probabilistic manner by operating in conjunction with a wide variety of biological and psychosocial developmental factors and life experiences. To consider the whole person (that is, to reintegrate sexual development into human development), we need to apply a developmental systems perspective to both the definition of healthy female sexuality and our investigations of the processes that lead to healthy outcomes. The following sections describe basic concepts of a developmental systems approach and suggest illustrative directions for future research within this framework.

A Developmental Systems Approach to the Study of Adolescent Female Sexual Development

A developmental systems approach (Gottlieb, 1998) specifies that the processes that "cause" development reflect the coactions of two or more factors working within and across the levels of the system: biological levels (for example, genetic, neural), a behavioral level, and an environmental level (cultural, social, and physical). These coactional processes are bidirectional. Processes at the "lower" biological levels have the capacity to change elements or process at "higher" levels, such as cognition and behavior, and processes at the higher levels in turn can affect factors and process at lower levels. However, simply incorporating elements from different levels is inadequate for a developmental analysis. Rather, it is necessary to specify hypothesized coacting factors and their coactional processes. (See Gottlieb, 1998, and Gottlieb & Halpern, 2002, for elaboration and examples.) The WHO definition of sexual health lends itself to a developmental systems model in its specification that sexual health is not just physical but also psychological and social, and in its assumption that particular aspects of the cultural and physical environments are necessary conditions for sexual health.

One implication of adopting the elements of the WHO definition of female sexual health is that research must add more systematic studies of motivational and socioemotional dimensions to the traditional health outcomes of physical disease, freedom from sexual coercion, risk taking, and basic reproductive health. For example, little is known about arousal-seeking behavior and the role of physical pleasure in female sexuality (Wallen, 1995), and there are no developmental analyses of these topics for adolescent girls. Given the importance of psychological and emotional intimacy for female sexuality, a better understanding of the interconnections between the physical and socioemotional aspects of sexual development is needed.

How can a developmental systems approach inform the goal of integrating physical and psychosocial aspects of sexual health? The balance of this chapter discusses two themes for future work. The focus here, given the chapter's charge, is on biological elements. However, the themes relate to both within-level and across-level analyses, with an eye toward the bidirectional processes and dynamic nature of developmental systems. The themes are to (1) integrate multiple biological factors in developmental analyses of adolescent female sexuality and (2) pay more attention to the top-down aspect of bidirectional processes in the developmental system, that is, the contributions of life experiences, or learning, to biological process and long-term sexual health.

Expand the Scope of Biological Factors, and Consider Their Coactional Contributions to Sexual Development. Endocrine, genetic, and neural systems are tightly intertwined and bidirectional in effects. Hormones turn on genes, and gene expression (or lack thereof) contributes to individual differences in sensitivity to hormones. Increasing appreciation of the complex interactions between the nervous and endocrine systems and knowledge about brain restructuring during adolescence have increased attention to neural factors in maturation (Sisk & Foster, 2004). These complex coactional processes would represent a more dynamic approach to biological issues and should be a target for research in healthy sexuality. Illustrative possibilities are suggested.

Consider Hormones of Potentially Special Relevance to Female Sexuality. Investigations of hormonal contributions to sexuality in humans have focused largely on gonadal and adrenal steroids. However, the importance of emotional, affiliative, and intimate interpersonal interactions in female sexuality points to at least two other hormones, with balancing or opposing properties, that merit additional attention: neuropeptides (for example, oxytocin) and glucocorticoids (for example, cortisol).

Oxytocin, produced in the hypothalamus, is important in lactation and parturition. It is also purported to be important in affiliative behavior (Insel, 1992), and its potential sexual effects were recognized in the 1980s (Argiolas, 1999). Data from animal models suggest a facilitative role in sexual motivation, excitement, and orgasm. Although most work on oxytocin and sexuality is based on animal models, human data also support associations between oxytocin and various facets of sexual response and function, such as vaginal lubrication (Anderson-Hunt & Dennerstein, 1994, 1995; Salonia et al., 2005) and muscular contractions during orgasm (Argiolis & Melis, 2003; Blaicher et al., 1999; Carmichael et al., 1987). One case study suggests that oxytocin may be associated with sexual desire, possibly with enhanced contributions in the presence of sex-steroid hormones (Anderson-Hunt & Dennerstein, 1995).

Oxytocin may be of special interest to developmental analyses of female sexuality because positive social interactions, including physical touch and emotional intimacy, have been linked with oxytocin release, and release of oxytocin appears to be conditionable. Positive social experiences and memories, both somatic and psychological, can reactivate oxytocin-based physiological responses (Uvnäs-Moberg, 1998). In addition, oxytocin inhibits secretion of glucocorticoids, which are stress hormones (Chiodera & Salvarani, 1991) and therefore may play a role in the stress-protective effects of positive social interactions (Uvnäs-Moberg, 1998). Associations among oxytocin levels, positive affect, and orgasm (Carmichael et al., 1994; Turner et al., 1999) along with oxytocin's inhibitory relationship with stress hormones suggest bidirectional pathways through which oxytocin could contribute to sexual motivation and subjective experiences of sexual pleasure, and through which life experiences (sexual and nonsexual positive interactions, and resulting pleasure) could alter biology (for example, stress hormone activity and neuroendocrine maturation) and the experience of sexuality.

The establishment of constructive and satisfying romantic relationships is a key developmental task of adolescence and an important aspect of sexual health. However, involvement in romantic and sexual relationships has been associated with elevated depressive symptoms for girls (Brooks, Harris, Thrall, & Woods, 2002; Burge, Felts, Chenier, & Parrillo, 1995). Gradual rises in cortisol levels in early adolescence, combined with decreased serotonin levels and increased dopamine activity, and other changes in the brain have led some researchers to suggest that adolescence is a period of heightened stress sensitivity (Kiess et al., 1995; Spear, 2000; Walker, 2002). The association between romantic involvement and depressive affect may be one manifestation of heightened stress sensitivity and indicates a need for better information about the qualities of romantic relationships and how they may contribute to emotional aspects of sexual health. Biological mechanisms involving oxytocin and stress hormones could play a role in this process. The beneficial effects of positive social interactions, and the association between emotional and physical intimacy and oxytocin release, suggest that engagement in emotionally positive intimate relationships could lead to repeated oxytocin release (Uvnäs-Moberg, 1998), thereby facilitating pleasure, psychological adaptation, and reduction of stress hormones (Carter & Altemus, 1997). This top-down process could then feed back to continued positive social interactions. Thus, considering multiple hormonal systems, in conjunction with multiple aspects of romantic and sexual experience, could inform our understanding of pathways to positive developmental outcomes.

Consider Genetic and Neural Contributions. Multiple biometrical (behavioral genetic) studies suggest genetic contributions to aspects of sexual behavior traditionally studied by adolescent health researchers, such as age at first coitus (Dunne et al., 1997; Martin, Eaves, & Eysenck, 1977; Miller et al., 1999; Rodgers, Rowe, & Buster, 1999), fertility expectations (Rodgers & Doughty, 2000), and childbearing motivations (Pasta & Miller, 2000). However, little research to date has used molecular genetic approaches (investigating the functional implications of polymorphisms or different forms of alleles) to sexuality, particularly adolescent sexuality. Dopamine polymorphisms may be especially relevant to sexuality because dopamine is an important catecholamine neurotransmitter that plays a role in arousing motivational systems. There are two classes of dopamine receptors: D1-like (D1 and D5) and D2-like (D2, D3, and D4). Animal models indicate that dopamine is facilitative of sexual activity (Hull et al., 1999; Melis & Argiolas, 1995; van Furth, Wolterink, & van Rhee, 1995). Dopamine also has peripheral functions, such as moderating hormone secretion. In human work, Miller et al. (1999) reported a significant interaction between two dopamine receptor polymorphisms (D1 and D2) and age at first sex, and Guo and Tong (2005) reported an association between the D4 three-repeat polymorphism and having first sex during adolescence versus early adulthood.

There is a large volume of work (with mixed findings; see Wong, Buckle, & Van Tol, 2000, for a review) examining links between variations in the D4 receptor and the personality trait of novelty or sensation seeking, a trait that may have significant implications for adolescent romantic styles and sexuality. Most of the research to date has been limited to investigations of bivariate relationships, and more complex coactional processes between developmental histories, proximal life experiences related to sexuality, and multiple genetic polymorphisms have not been explored. For example, another neurotransmitter, serotonin, has inhibitory effects, and reduced serotonergic transmission could contribute to decreased impulse control. Interactions between dopamine and serotonin polymorphisms (Ebstein et al., 1997) may have implications for psychosocial unconventionality and, thus, patterns of romantic and sexual behavior (Halpern, 2003). These more complex approaches to the study of gene-environmental contributions to sexual development, and the incorporation of measures of gene expression, have not been implemented in research to date, but could elucidate the integrative contributions of multiple biological factors to sexual development.

Direct More Research to Top-Down Processes in the Developmental System. The hormone studies described earlier illustrate investigations of direct hormonal contributions to sexual motivation and behavior and constitute the bulk of this research area. However, the hormone behavior literature also includes demonstrations of behavioral and contextual effects on hormone levels. For example, sexual activity can raise testosterone levels (Pirke,

Kockott, & Dittmar, 1974; Helhammer, Hubert, & Schurmeyer, 1985), and stressful experiences can raise cortisol levels while simultaneously lowering testosterone and causing androgen receptors to become unavailable (Burnstein, Maiorinao, & Cameron, 1995; Cumming, Quigley, & Yen, 1983; Sapolsky, 1991). There have also been demonstrations of how top-down processes may be linked to sexual patterns. For example, physiological "reactors" to stressful contexts have fewer sexual partners, but because of the stressful nature of contraception negotiation, they are less likely to use contraception consistently (Halpern, Campbell, Agnew, Thompson, & Udry, 2002).

Top-down processes are especially intriguing in the light of the significant neural changes that occur during adolescence. Work using magnetic resonance imaging (MRI) and functional MRI has documented the extensive refinement of "brain architecture" that occurs throughout adolescence and into adulthood. (See Weinberger, Elvevag, & Giedd, 2005, for a description of these changes.) Neural connections are vastly expanded, becoming increasingly complex, and unused or ineffective connections are pruned back. Pruning may ultimately contribute to impulse control by lowering the amount of excitatory stimulation reaching the cortex. In addition to changes in neural connections, there is increasing myelination of axons. Myelin is a fatty chemical coat that increases the speed and efficiency of neural conduction across regions of the brain (Weinberger et al., 2005). Cells that carry dopamine become more robust, a change likely related to increasingly mature thinking and impulse control across adolescence. There is an increase in focal activation or processing for specific tasks rather than more generalized activation, and improved abilities for parallel processing across the two brain hemispheres. Most of these changes occur in the prefrontal cortex, the seat of executive function and the controller of lower brain centers related to impulsivity, memory, and emotion. It is likely that the hormonal changes of puberty, such as increases in testosterone and estrogen, play a role in activating genes involved in these cellular changes (Weinberger et al., 2005) and that steroids contribute to additional organization of neural circuits that play a role in sexuality (Sisk & Foster, 2004). These contributions of pubertal hormones to structural changes in neural connections (Giedd et al., 1999) illustrate the blurring of traditional distinctions between organizational and activational (that is, eliciting process) effects of hormones, and highlight the dynamic and bidirectional nature of the developmental system.

Since its social construction (Crockett, 1997), adolescence has been viewed as a time of learning and experimentation directed at preparation for adulthood. Such experimentation is adaptive for emotional and cognitive growth (Chrousos, 1998), albeit potentially risky. If adolescence is a sensitive period in terms of increased brain plasticity or stress sensitivity, or both, then positive life experiences, including those relating to sexuality, may have enhanced effects on an increasingly adaptive brain.

Our understanding of changes in the brain during adolescence is at an early stage, and it is not clear whether and how brain imaging maps brain function. However, the "best hypothesis at present is that learning and the formation of memories guide the building up of [neural] connections" (Weinberger et al., 2005, p. 12). If this hypothesis is correct, then experience will determine brain structure, which in turn will affect adolescent decision making, risk taking, and perceptions about what is rewarding, both physically and psychologically. This means that investigations of sexual socialization experiences that have the theoretical potential to literally build the brain assume even greater significance for our understanding of adolescent sexuality and its implications for long-term sexual functioning and health. Given the interconnections among hormonal, genetic, and neural systems, the hypothesis also suggests that the timing of experiences, and perhaps their sequences, may be important to brain organization, and therefore merit additional attention. Socialization factors play a large role in the meaning attached to sexual activities and also affect sexual expression through contributions to biology and sexual response (what is pleasurable, aversive, and so forth). If there is continuity in sexual patterns from adolescence into adulthood, their biological underpinnings and contributions may be largely shaped during adolescence.

Conclusion

We have little information about how sexual experience and sexual health in adolescence translate into sexual health in adulthood. It is not even clear whether adolescent and adult sexual health should be defined in the same or different ways, based on developmental and cultural considerations. The inclusion of the cultural environment in the concept of sexual health not only implicates interactions with culture as a driving force of development, it also indicates that the very definition of sexual health is embedded in national, political, and cultural contexts. It may not be possible to achieve full consensus on a definition of sexual health or on the processes that should be facilitated to achieve sexual health (Giami, 2002). The possibility that sexual experimentation and socialization during adolescence could make such fundamental contributions to the neurobiology underlying sexual health raises profound social policy issues about adolescent education, guidance, and control. Attempts to address these issues should be informed by the results of scientific investigations that consider the full range of factors and process in the developmental system and that approach the adolescent girl as a whole person.

References

Adams, D. B., Gold, A. R., & Burt, A. D. (1978). Rise in female sexual activity at ovulation blocked by oral contraceptives. *New England Journal of Medicine, 299,* 1145–1150.

Agmo, A. (1999). Sexual motivation—an inquiry into events determining the occurrence of sexual behavior. *Behavioral Brain Research, 105,* 129–150.

Anderson-Hunt, M., & Dennerstein, L. (1994). Increased female sexual response after oxytocin. *British Medical Journal, 309,* 929.

Anderson-Hunt, M., & Dennerstein, L. (1995). Oxytocin and female sexuality. *Gynecological and Obstetrical Investigation, 40,* 217–221.

Argiolis, A. (1999). Neuropeptides and sexual behavior. *Neuroscience and Biobehavioral Reviews, 23,* 1127–1142.

Argiolis, A., & Melis, M. R. (2003). The neurophysiology of the sexual cycle. *Journal of Endocrinological Investigation, 26,* 20–22.

Bancroft, J. (2005). The endocrinology of sexual arousal. *Journal of Endocrinology, 186,* 411–427.

Bancroft, J., Sanders, D., Davidson, D., & Warner, P. (1983). Mood, sexuality, hormones and the menstrual cycle: III. Sexuality and the role of androgens. *Psychosomatic Medicine, 45,* 509-516.

Beach, F. A. (1976). Sexual attractivity, proceptivity, and receptivity in female mammals. *Hormones and Behavior, 7,* 105–138.

Becker, J. B., Breedlove, S. M., & Crews, D. (1992). *Behavioral endocrinology.* Cambridge, MA: MIT Press.

Blaicher, W., Gruber, D., Bieglmayer, C., Blaicher, A. M., Knogler, W., & Huber, J. C. (1999). The role of oxytocin in relation to female sexual arousal. *Gynecologic and Obstetric Investigation, 47,* 125–126.

Boling, J. L., & Blandau, R. J. (1939). The estrogen-progesterone induction of mating responses in the spayed female rat. *Endocrinology, 25,* 359–364.

Brooks, T. L., Harris, S. K., Thrall, J. S., & Woods, E. R. (2002). Association of adolescent risk behaviors with mental health symptoms in high school students. *Journal of Adolescent Health, 31,* 240–246.

Brooks-Gunn, J., & Reiter, E. O. (1990). The role of pubertal processes. In S. S. Feldman & G. R. Elliott (Eds.), *At the threshold: The developing adolescent* (pp. 16–53). Cambridge, MA: Harvard University Press.

Bullough, V. L. (1994). *Science in the bedroom: A history of sex research.* New York: Basic Books.

Burge, V., Felts, M., Chenier, T., & Parrillo, A. V. (1995). Drug use, sexual activity, and suicidal behavior in U.S. high school students. *Journal of School Health, 65,* 222–227.

Burnstein, K. L., Maiorinao, J. L., & Cameron, D. J. (1995). Androgen and glucocorticoid regulation and androgen receptor cDNA expression. *Molecular and Cell Endocrinology, 115,* 177–186.

Carmichael, M. S., Humbert, R., Dixen, J., Plamisano, G., Greenleaf, W., & Davidson, J. M. (1987). Plasma oxytocin increases in the human sexual response. *Journal of Clinical Endocrinology and Metabolism, 64,* 27–31.

Carter, C. S., & Altemus, M. (1997). Integrative functions of lactational hormones in social behavior and stress management. *Annals of the New York Academy of Science, 807,* 164–174.

Chiodera, P., & Salvarani, C. (1991). Relationship between plasma profiles of oxytocin and adrenocorticotropic hormone during suckling or breast stimulation in women. *Hormones and Research, 35,* 119–123.

Chrousos, G. P. (1998). Stressors, stress, and neuroendocrine integration of the adaptive response. *Annals of the New York Academy of Sciences, 851,* 311–335.

Crockett, L. J. (1997). Cultural, historical, and subcultural contexts of adolescence: Implications for health and development. In J. Schulenberg, J. L. Maggs, & K. Hurrelmann (Eds.), *Health risks and developmental transitions during adolescence* (pp. 23–53). Cambridge: Cambridge University Press.

Cumming, D. C., Quigley, M. E., & Yen, S.S.C. (1983). Acute suppression of circulating testosterone levels by cortisol in men. *Journal of Clinical Endocrinology and Metabolism, 57,* 671–673.

Davis, S. R. (1998). The clinical use of androgens in female sexual disorders. *Journal of Sex and Marital Therapy, 24,* 153–163.

Dennerstein, L., Gotts, G., Brown, J. B., Morse, C. A., Farley, T.M.M., & Pinol, A. (1994). The relationship between the menstrual cycle and female sexual interest in women with PMS complaints and volunteers. *Psychoneuroendocrinology, 19,* 293–304.

Dunne, M. P., Martin, N. G., Statham, D. J., Slutske, W. S., Dinwiddie, S. H., Bucholz, K. K., Madden, P.A.F., & Heath, A. C. (1997). Genetic and environmental contributions to variance in age at first sexual intercourse. *Psychological Science, 8,* 211–216.

Ebstein, R. P., Segman, R., Benjamin, J., Osher, Y., Nemanov, L., & Belmaker, R. H. (1997). 5-HT2c (HTR2C) serotonin receptor gene polymorphism associated with the human personality trait of reward dependence: Interaction with dopamine D4 receptor (D4DR) and dopamine D3 (D3DR) polymorphisms. *American Journal of Medical Genetics (Neuropsychiatric Genetics), 74,* 65–72.

Ehrhardt, A. (1996). Editorial: Our view of adolescent sexuality—A focus on risk behavior without the developmental context. *American Journal of Public Health, 86,* 1523–1525.

Finkelstein, J. W., Susman, E. J., Chinchilli, V. M., D'Arcangelo, M. R., Kunselman, S. J., Schwab, J., Demers, L. M., Liben, L. S., & Kulin, H. E. (1998). Effects of estrogen or testosterone on self-reported sexual responses and behaviors in hypogonadal adolescents. *Journal of Clinical Endocrinology and Metabolism, 83,* 2281–2285.

Giami, A. (2002). Sexual health: The emergence, development, and diversity of a concept. *Annual Review of Sex Research, 13,* 1–35.

Giedd, J. N., Blumenthal, J., Jeffries, N. O., Castellanos, F. X., Liu, H., Zijdenbos, A., Paus, T., Evans, A. C., & Rapoport, J. L. (1999). Brain development during childhood and adolescence: A longitudinal MRI study. *Nature Neuroscience, 2,* 861–863.

Gottlieb, G. (1998). Normally occurring environmental and behavioral influences on gene activity: From central dogma to probabilistic epigenesis. *Psychological Review, 105,* 792–802.

Gottlieb, G., & Halpern, C. T. (2002). A relational view of causality in normal and abnormal development. *Development and Psychopathology, 14,* 421–435.

Guo, G., & Tong, Y. (2005). *Age at first sexual intercourse, genes, and social and demographic context: Evidence from twins and the dopamine D4 receptor gene.* Unpublished manuscript.

Halpern, C. T. (2003). Biological influences on adolescent romantic and sexual behavior. In P. Florsheim (Ed.), *Adolescent romantic relations and sexual behavior: Theory, research, and practical implications* (pp. 57–84). Mahwah, NJ: Erlbaum.

Halpern, C. T., Campbell, B., Agnew, C. R., Thompson, V., & Udry, J. R. (2002). Associations between stress reactivity and sexual and non-sexual risk taking in adolescent males. *Hormones and Behavior, 42,* 387–398.

Halpern, C. T., Udry, J. R., & Suchindran, C. (1997). Testosterone predicts initiation of coitus in adolescent females. *Psychosomatic Medicine, 59,* 161–171.

Harvey, S. M. (1987). Female sexual behavior: Fluctuations during the menstrual cycle. *Journal of Psychosomatic Research, 31,* 101–110.

Helhammer, D. H., Hubert, W., & Schurmeyer, J. (1985). Changes in saliva testosterone after psychological stimulation in men. *Psychoneuroendocrinology, 14,* 266–274.

Herdt, G., & Boxer, A. (1993). *Children of horizons.* Boston: Beacon Press.

Herdt, G., & McClintock, M. (2000). The magical age of 10. *Archives of Sexual Behavior, 29,* 587–606.

Hull, E. M., Lorrain, D. S., Du, V., Matuszewich, L., Lumley, L. A., Putnam, S. K., & Moses, J. (1999). Hormone-neurotransmitter interactions in the control of sexual behavior. *Behavioral Brain Research, 105,* 105–116.

Insel, T. R. (1992). Oxytocin—a neuropeptide for affiliation: Evidence from behavioral, receptor autoradiographic, and comparative studies. *Psychoneuroendocrinology, 17,* 3–35.

Kiess, W., Meidert, A., Dressendorfer, R., Scheiver, K., Kessler, U., & Konig, A. (1995). Salivary cortisol levels throughout childhood and adolescence. *Pediatric Research, 37,* 502–506.

Martin, N. G., Eaves, L. J., & Eysenck, H. J. (1977). Genetical, environmental, and personality factors influencing the age of first sexual intercourse in twins. *Journal of Biosocial Science, 9,* 91–97.

Matteo, S., & Rissman, E. F. (1984). Increased sexual activity during the midcycle portion of the human menstrual cycle. *Hormones and Behavior, 18,* 249–255.

McClintock, M. K., & Adler, N. T. (1978). The role of the female during copulation in wild and domestic Norway rats (*Rattus norvegicus*). *Behaviour, 67,* 67–96.

McClintock, M. K., & Herdt, G. (1996). Rethinking puberty: The development of sexual attraction. *Current Directions in Psychological Science, 5,* 179–183.

Melis, M. R., & Argiolas, A. (1995). Dopamine and sexual behavior. *Neuroscience and Biobehavioral Reviews, 19,* 19–38.

Meuwissen, I., & Over, R. (1992). Sexual arousal across phases of the human menstrual cycle. *Archives of Sexual Behavior, 21,* 165–173.

Miller, W. B., Pasta, D. J., Macmurray, J. C., Chiu, C., Wu, H., & Comings, D. E. (1999). Dopamine receptor genes are associated with age at first sexual intercourse. *Journal of Biosocial Science, 31,* 43–54.

Palmer, J. D., Udry, J. R., & Morris, N. M. (1982). Diurnal and weekly, but no lunar rhythms in human copulation. *Human Biology, 54,* 111–121.

Pasta, D. J., & Miller, W. B. (2000). A heritability study of childbearing motivation. In J. L. Rodgers, D. C. Rowe, & W. B. Miller (Eds.), *Genetic influences on human fertility and sexuality: Theoretical and empirical contributions from the biological and behavioral sciences* (pp. 107–120). Norwell, MA: Kluwer .

Pattatuci, A., & Hamer, D. (1995). Developmental and familiarity of sexual orientation in females. *Behavioral Genetics, 25,* 407–420.

Pfaus, J. G. (1996). Homologies of animal and human sexual behaviors. *Hormones and Behavior, 30,* 187–200.

Pirke, K., Kockott, G., & Dittmar, F. (1974). Psychosexual stimulation and plasma testosterone in man. *Archives of Sexual Behavior, 3,* 577–584.

Rodgers, J. L., & Doughty, D. (2000). Genetic and environmental influences on fertility expectations and outcomes using NLSY kinship data. In J. L. Rodgers, D. C. Rowe, & W. B. Miller (Eds.) *Genetic influences on human fertility and sexuality: Theoretical and empirical contributions from the biological and behavioral sciences* (pp. 85–105). Norwell, MA: Kluwer.

Rodgers, J. L., Rowe, D. C., & Buster, M. (1999). Nature, nurture and first sexual intercourse in the USA: Fitting behavioral genetic models to NLSY kinship data. *Journal of Biosocial Science, 31,* 29–41.

Salonia, A., Nappi, R. E., Pontillo, M., Daverio, R., Smeraldi, A., Briganti, A., Fabbri, F., Zanni, G., Rigatti, P., & Montorsi, F. (2005). Menstrual cycle-related changes in plasma oxytocin are relevant to normal sexual function in healthy women. *Hormones and Behavior, 47,* 164–169.

Sapolsky, R. M. (1991). Testicular function, social rank, and personality among wild baboons. *Psychoneuroendocrinology, 16,* 281–301.

Satcher, D. (2001). *The surgeon general's call to action to promote sexual health and responsible sexual behavior.* Washington, D.C.: U.S. Department of Health and Human Services.

Savin-Williams, R. C., & Diamond, L. M. (2000). Sexual identity trajectories among sexual-minority youths: Gender comparisons. *Archives of Sexual Behavior, 29,* 607–627.

Sexuality Information and Education Council of the United States. (1995). *Consensus statement from the National Commission on Adolescent Sexual Health.* New York: Author.

Sherwin, B. B., & Gelfand, M. M. (1987). The role of androgen in the maintenance of sexual functioning in oophorectomized women. *Psychosomatic Medicine, 49,* 397–409.

Sherwin, B. B., Gelfand, M. M., & Brender, W. (1985). Androgen enhances sexual motivation in females: A prospective, crossover study of sex steroid administration in surgical menopause. *Psychosomatic Medicine, 47,* 339–351.

Shifren, J. L., Braunstein, G. D., Simon, J. A., Casson, P. R., Buster, J. E., Redmond, G. P., Burki, R. E., Ginsburg, E. S., Rosen, R. C., Leiblum, S. R., Caramelli, K. E., Mazer, N. A., Jones K. P., & Daugherty, C. A. (2000). Transdermal testosterone treatment in women with impaired sexual function after oophorectomy. *New England Journal of Medicine, 343,* 682–688.

Sisk, C. L., & Foster, D. L. (2004). The neural basis of puberty and adolescence. *Nature Neuroscience, 7,* 1040–1047.

Spear, L. P. (2000). The adolescent brain and age-related behavioral manifestations. *Neuroscience and Biobehavioral Reviews, 24,* 417–463.

Stanislaw, H., & Rice, F. J. (1988). Correlation between sexual desire and menstrual cycle characteristics. *Archives of Sexual Behavior, 17,* 499–508.

Starling, E. H. (1905). Croonian Lecture: On the chemical correlation of the functions of the body I. *Lancet, 2,* 339–341.

Tolman, D. L., Striepe, M. I., & Harmon, T. (2003). Gender matters: Constructing a model of adolescent sexual health. *Journal of Sex Research, 40,* 4–12.

Turner, R.A., Altemus, M., Enos, T., Cooper, B., & McGuinness, T. (1999). Preliminary research on plasma oxytocin in normal cycling women: Investigating emotion and interpersonal distress. *Psychiatry, 62,* 97–113.

Udry, J. R., Talbert, L. M., & Morris, N. M. (1986). Biosocial foundations for adolescent female sexuality. *Demography, 23,* 217–230.

Uvnäs-Moberg, K. (1998). Oxytocin may mediate the benefits of positive social interactions and emotions. *Psychoneuroendocrinology, 23,* 819–835.

van Furth, W. R., Wolterink, G., & van Rhee, J. M. (1995). Regulation of masculine sexual behavior: Involvement of brain opioids and dopamine. *Brain Research Reviews, 21,* 162–184.

Wallen, K. (1995). The evolution of female sexual desire. In P. Abramson & S. Pinkerton (Eds.), *Sexual nature, sexual culture* (pp. 57–79). Chicago: University of Chicago Press.

Walker, E. F. (2002). Adolescent neurodevelopment and psychopathology. *Current Directions in Psychological Science, 11,* 24–28.

Weinberger, D. R., Elvevag, B., & Giedd, J. N. (2005). *The adolescent brain: A work in progress.* Washington, D.C.: National Campaign to Prevent Teen Pregnancy. www.teenpregnancy.org/resources/reading/pdf/BRAIN.pdf.

Wong, A.H.C, Buckle, C. E., & Van Tol, H.H.M. (2000). Polymorphisms in dopamine receptors: What do they tell us? *European Journal of Pharmacology, 410,* 183–203.

World Health Organization. (1946, June 19–22). *Preamble to the constitution of the World Health Organization as adopted by the International Health Conference.* New York: Author.

World Health Organization. (1975). Education and treatment in human sexuality: The training of health professionals (Technical Report Series No. 572). Geneva: World Health Organization.

World Health Organization. Regional Office for Europe. (1987). *Concepts of sexual health: Report of a working group.* http://whqlibdoc.who.int/euro/-1993/EUR_ICP_MCH_521.pdf.

CAROLYN TUCKER HALPERN is an associate professor in the Department of Maternal and Child Health, School of Public Health, University of North Carolina at Chapel Hill.

NEW DIRECTIONS FOR CHILD AND ADOLESCENT DEVELOPMENT • DOI: 10.1002/cad

The psychosocial impact of puberty on changes in girls' feelings about their bodies and their sexuality is discussed. We present a model of girls' sexuality development that incorporates puberty, self, and peer systems.

Puberty and Girls' Sexuality: Why Hormones Are Not the Complete Answer

Julia A. Graber, Lisa M. Sontag

Although puberty is often considered a biological event in development, it occurs in a social context. In addition, puberty influences girls' development, especially emerging sexuality, through personal reappraisal and social feedback, as well as hormonal input. This chapter focuses on the psychological and social impacts of pubertal development on changes in girls' feelings about themselves (their bodies) and their sexuality. These issues are discussed in terms of sexual feelings, sense of self as a sexual being, and sexual behaviors as central components in how girls regulate and express their sexuality.

Puberty and sexual development are, by definition, connected: the processes that comprise pubertal development result in the attainment of reproductive capability in nearly all individuals (excluding the relatively rare cases of disorders of puberty). As such, the neuroendocrine changes that set in motion hormonal activity, which result in development of reproductive organs, along with growth in height and weight, all combine to produce reproductive capacity; that is, girls' bodies are not only able to become pregnant but also to sustain pregnancy and subsequent lactation. Hence, by the end of puberty, focusing strictly on the demands of the species to continue, girls are ready to have sex and reproduce.

In industrialized societies today, girls attain the initial capacity for reproduction at about twelve and a half years of age, the average age of having

NEW DIRECTIONS FOR CHILD AND ADOLESCENT DEVELOPMENT, no. 112, Summer 2006   © Wiley Periodicals, Inc.
Published online in Wiley InterScience (www.interscience.wiley.com) • DOI: 10.1002/cd.160

one's first menstrual cycle in the United States (Herman-Giddens et al., 1997). However, for most girls, it will take another two years before the menstrual cycle is mature and girls' fertility is more stable (Grumbach & Styne, 1998). Clearly, in these same industrialized societies, girls are strongly discouraged from starting to reproduce at fourteen or fifteen years of age. In the United States, a majority of girls will have intercourse by age seventeen to eighteen in mid- to late adolescence (Alan Guttmacher Institute, 2001), even though they are discouraged from engaging in intercourse and reproduction. Thus, puberty confers a capacity that is linked to sexual behavior, but this capacity has little connection to actual behavior in and of itself.

Hence, the most basic questions for this discussion are why and how a psychological construct such as sexuality develops at all. What does it mean to develop sexuality beyond reproduction? And in terms of puberty and sexuality, is it even likely that something that happens to everyone in the early phase of adolescence will translate into longer-term trajectories for behavior? This discussion provides some thoughts on the role of puberty in answering these questions. For these purposes, we, like many others, have noted that sexuality is more than simply first intercourse or sexual "risks"; rather, it encompasses feelings about oneself, reappraisals of the self, attitudes, and behaviors (Graber, Brooks-Gunn, & Galen, 1998).

Certainly given the risks to present and long-term health of some sexual behaviors (for example, failure to use condoms), the plethora of studies on sexual risk is warranted. At the same time, there is still a dearth of investigation of normative sexual development, with exceptions noted in this volume. Moreover, as noted in theories of developmental psychopathology, it is likely that the examination of risk would be informed by an understanding of healthy sexual development (Masten & Curtis, 2000). Prevention strategies are likely to have the highest payoff if they incorporate factors that not only protect against risk but also promote healthy development (Graber, Nichols, Lynne, Brooks-Gunn, & Botvin, in press). However, to date, such principles have not guided research on sexuality, and it is often difficult to articulate what the development of healthy sexuality is. Most often healthy development is defined as the absence of risk. While such a definition might represent the minimal standard, it does not reflect the complexities of girls' development and how girls construct a positive or healthy sense of themselves as sexual beings. Unfortunately, in our discussion of how puberty may be associated with the development of sexuality in girls, we too found ourselves inferring healthy trajectories from what is known about unhealthy trajectories.

Our Model

In our approach to adolescent sexuality, we focus specifically on puberty and how it is experienced personally and in a social context. For the sake of discussion, we present two complementary models for links between puberty and sexuality. The first model indicates that sexual desires and

NEW DIRECTIONS FOR CHILD AND ADOLESCENT DEVELOPMENT • DOI: 10.1002/cad

behaviors are in part the result of brain development and physiological processes (see Figure 3.1). Sexual behaviors are linked to brain processes that control pleasure and behavior (McKenna, 2001). In addition, the brain, specifically the hypothalamus, in connection with the pituitary, gonadal, and adrenal glands, is central to puberty and eventual reproductive capacity. Interestingly, although pubertal hormonal changes appear to influence the development of interest in sexual activity and subsequent sexual behaviors (see Chapter Two, this volume), effects are often not large and are typically moderated by other factors.

In part, puberty influences the development of sexuality through effects on feelings about the self, especially feelings about one's developing body, and how such changes are experienced in social milieus, especially peer groups and interpersonal relationships (Brooks-Gunn, Graber, & Paikoff, 1994). Girls themselves likely use their own physical maturity in reevaluating their sense of themselves as sexual beings. Sexual behaviors appear to increase with increases in the external changes of puberty (Flannery, Rowe, & Gulley, 1993; Udry & Campbell, 1994), although effects do not appear to be pervasive. The timing of puberty—that is, going through puberty earlier, at the same time, or later than one's peers—has more often been linked to sexual behavior. An extensive review of this literature by Ellis (2004) indicated that among girls, earlier maturation was associated with younger ages of first intercourse, earlier onset of dating behaviors, and adolescent pregnancy. However, some studies have suggested that these effects are more often found among subgroups of girls and hence vary by context, race, and ethnicity (Cavanagh, 2004). Our goal is to explore why these associations may or may not be found by looking at sexual behaviors as part of a broader developmental process.

Hence, the primary focus of our discussion is on the processes outlined in Figure 3.2. In particular, we suggest that aspects of the self system (for example, body image and emotional adjustment) that are developing prior to puberty have bidirectional (or interactive) associations with puberty. In addition, we suggest that social contexts such as same-gender and other-gender relationships and peer groups that influence development prior to puberty also have bidirectional associations with the self system and hence the social experience of puberty. Each of these factors—puberty, self, and social context—is salient to the development of sexuality.

Figure 3.1. A Simple Model for the Physiological Processes of Puberty and Links to Sexuality

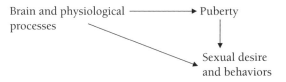

Figure 3.2. A Psychosocial Model for the Role of Puberty in the Development of Sexuality

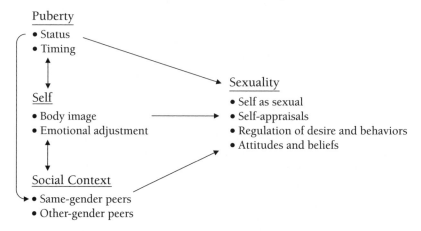

Of course, other components of self and social contexts are connected with sexuality. For example, an extensive literature has focused on parents and family context and their connections to adolescent sexual behaviors, although less work has focused on sexuality separate from sexual risks. Hence, family factors could be added to our model but are not considered in this discussion (see Chapter Four, this volume, for a discussion of family communication issues).

In line with prior work, we have adopted a view of sexuality that has multiple components, begins to develop more fully during puberty, develops extensively over adolescence, and is interconnected with changes in self and social context during this period (Graber et al., 1998; Graber, Britto, & Brooks-Gunn, 1999). As such, sexuality is likely to have important connections to engagement in sexual behaviors and experiences, which in turn stimulate reevaluation of beliefs and attitudes about one's sexuality.

Self and the Development of Body Image

As articulated by Buzwell and Rosenthal (1996), a sexual self incorporates feelings about or evaluation of one's appearance. If sexuality is so highly related to how we feel about our appearance, the first issue that should be addressed is why people care about how they look. Isn't a large part of this concern, especially during and after puberty, due to an increased desire for others, especially potential sexual partners, to find us attractive? Because of a shift in peer contexts and the increase in sexual interest in others, adolescent girls (at least girls with heterosexual interests) become hyperaware of what makes them attractive to boys. During adolescence, girls not only become more aware of appearance in relation to attracting boys, but they also begin to engage in social comparison at a more exaggerated level. In a sense, they become aware of their "competition" and begin to incorporate social comparison in evaluations and feelings about their appearance. Taught by media, friends, and family that a particular physique is attractive to the opposite sex, girls begin to evaluate their sexual attractiveness and their overall view of themselves based on these ideals.

Body image encompasses beliefs and feelings about, and representations of, one's body and its attributes, such as weight, size, and shape. The awareness of the social importance of appearance and the stigmas attached to differing from the norm or ideal emerge quite early in development. For example, Dohnt and Tiggemann (2004) found that over time, girls ages five to seven progressively preferred a thinner ideal figure compared to the larger figure they had chosen at younger ages; dieting awareness also increased over time. Ricciardelli, McCabe, and Holt (2003) reported that approximately 50 percent of the girls ages eight to eleven desired to be thinner, rated their weight as important, and endorsed weight-loss strategies. The fact that girls in elementary school are already concerned with dieting as a means to stay thin indicates that a thin ideal is learned over the course of the childhood years and is incorporated into self-assessments. As disconcerting as these findings may be, equally disconcerting is evidence that body image and ideations about body shape intensify as girls enter puberty.

Puberty and Body Image. The most drastic increase in body dissatisfaction for both boys and girls occurs around puberty (Graber, Petersen, & Brooks-Gunn, 1996). The onset of puberty brings about physical changes to the body that force individuals to reassess personal conceptions of their own body and how this fits into their existing conception of their self. During puberty, girls begin to experience fluctuations in hormones that influence the development of secondary sexual characteristics such as breasts, increase in lean muscle mass, and, most prominent for girls, an increase in body fat (Tanner, 1962). Puberty also has a social stimulus value in that others observe changes in girls' bodies, such as breast development or changes in hips and body shape, and subsequently alter how they interact with girls based on these observations. Due to these often dramatic appearance changes, most girls experience a downward trend in body image across early adolescence, when most girls are in the mid- to later stages of puberty (Graber et al., 1996).

The social and psychological experiences of puberty have generally been examined in terms of pubertal status and pubertal timing (Graber et al., 1996). Status refers to the current level of pubertal development that an individual has attained based on an indicator of pubertal development, such as breast development. Changes in status should affect all girls as they develop. For example, pubertal status indicators, such as an increase in body fat, are associated with increases in body dissatisfaction (Archibald, Graber, & Brooks-Gunn, 1999). But such changes appear to be limited to the pubertal years (Graber et al., 1996).

In contrast, pubertal timing—being earlier, later, or the same as peers—may play a more crucial role in the development of body image for adolescents (Graber et al., 1996; Williams & Currie, 2000). In general, off-time development has been hypothesized to be problematic for youth in that they may feel different from peers and hence have negative self-appraisals (Brooks-Gunn, Petersen, & Eichorn, 1985). In particular, early-maturing girls begin puberty earlier than most other girls or boys in their cohort and are most likely to feel different from peers and have negative self-appraisals. Because body image development relies heavily on social comparison of physical appearance, it comes as no surprise that adolescents who deviate from the mode with respect to puberty are at greater risk of developing body image concerns. We and our colleagues (Graber et al., 1996) have demonstrated that differential pathways exist for girls classified as either early, on time, or late in pubertal development. Specifically, improvements in body image are observed in mid-adolescence for on-time and late-maturing girls. For early-maturing girls, body satisfaction continues to drop throughout adolescence. Across studies, greater body dissatisfaction in girls in the postpubertal years is associated with earlier maturation (see Stice, 2003, for a review); often pubertal timing differences are not accounted for by actual differences in weight or body mass index, that is, weight accounting for height (Ohring, Graber, & Brooks-Gunn, 2002).

Pubertal timing and poor body image are also linked to more serious affective and behavioral disorders in girls, such as depression and eating disorders (see Graber, 2003, for a recent review), with impacts on adjustment into adulthood (Graber, Seeley, Brooks-Gunn, & Lewinsohn, 2004). Notably, depression and eating disorders are more prevalent in adolescent girls than boys, and at about the time that most girls have typically completed puberty (age fourteen), the gender differences in depression emerge (see Graber, 2004, for a recent review). Depressive problems are associated with disturbances in body image for girls but not boys (Allgood-Merten, Lewinsohn, & Hops, 1990). And body dissatisfaction is a symptom of eating disorders and has been found to predict increases in or onset of disordered eating in adolescent girls (see Stice, 2003, for a review). Moreover, Ohring and colleagues (2002) found that recurrent body dissatisfaction during adolescence was associated with earlier pubertal timing and predicted elevated depressive and eating symptoms in young adulthood.

Peer Relationships and Body Image. With evidence of increasing body image concerns during puberty, particularly for early-maturing girls, one issue is how feelings about the self, specifically appearance-related feelings, are shaped by social factors. Feelings of physical attractiveness directly affect an individual's sense of sexual efficacy when understanding and coping with oneself as a sexual being. Feelings of sexual attraction to others (Will others find me attractive?) are inherent factors in the development of feelings about one's sexuality.

Peers are particularly salient to appearance appraisals. Jones (2004) has found that girls who participated more often in appearance-focused conversations with peers were more likely to experience greater body dissatisfaction. Peer acceptance was also specifically based on acceptance by peers of one's appearance. In addition, heightened social comparison predicted increases in body dissatisfaction. These results suggest that girls who place greater emphasis on physical appearance, and in turn sexual attractiveness, are at greater risk for developing body image concerns. In addition, adolescent girls often use beliefs about the importance of appearance as a marker for group identification and social status. If adolescent girls are more likely to adopt appearance issues into their peer groups, and increased exposure to appearance-based conversations and appearance-based peer acceptance serve as risk factors for poor body image, then girls place themselves in a dangerous and circular pathway for poor self-appraisals.

In addition to peer group influences on body image, romantic relationships influence body image development. Compian, Gowen, and Hayward (2004) found that increasing levels of romantic involvement were associated with poorer body image among young adolescent girls. However, this effect was limited to Caucasian girls. In contrast, platonic involvement with boys was associated with positive body image. In another study, girls who placed high value on having a boyfriend also placed high value on physical attractiveness (Halpern, Udry, Campbell, & Suchindran, 1999). Interestingly in this same project, girls with higher body mass index were less likely to date, an association found even among girls who were not obese. These results suggest that girls' emphasis on physical appearance may in fact be a result of adolescent boys' desires to date girls who more closely resemble the thin ideal.

Implications for Positive Sexual Development. Overall, puberty and involvement with peers is related to body image development for adolescent girls. Additional investigation of the interconnections of puberty, peers, and self-appraisals is warranted in order to understand how different contexts shape girls' self-appraisals and their sexuality. With puberty comes new emotional experiences in terms of sexuality and changes in other emotions (for example, anger, and sadness). Some girls (for example, early maturers) clearly do not regulate these emotions as well as others. This has implications for sexual behaviors. Hypothetically, girls who are more effective regulators may be less likely to see themselves as different from peers (for example, on-time maturers) and may be less likely to immerse themselves in appearance-focused environments. Hence, it would be important to know if better emotion regulation is linked to better regulation of peer pressures, body image, and sexuality.

More important, only a subgroup of girls develops particularly negative self-appraisals. The typical experience is for girls to have declines in body image during puberty but then recover; many girls focus on attractiveness and appearance during early adolescence but do not develop eating problems or serious psychopathology. Moreover, most girls develop a sense of efficacy and positive appraisal of their sexual feelings, and sexual selves (Buzwell & Rosenthal, 1996). Hence, many girls are able to navigate developmental challenges. One subgroup that is less likely to have a positive trajectory is early maturers. Of course, pubertal timing is not a target for intervention. Thus, in order to improve the health trajectories for this group, the focus needs to be on why they are at risk. As we will discuss, one reason may be their involvement with romantic partners.

Also, in the light of concerns about childhood obesity, one challenge is framing messages around healthy eating and physical activity rather than the need to be thin or to diet to be desirable. This means combating multi-million-dollar dieting and advertising industries. Although we have not focused on family factors, parents provide protection from these influences, have the capacity to establish healthy practices early in life, and provide direct messages about body appraisals and health (Archibald et al., 1999). Unfortunately, parents may be uncomfortable dealing with the emotional changes, especially emerging sexual feelings, of adolescents and fail to tune into emotion regulation or body image problems.

Romantic Relationships

Changes in self-appraisals occur in connection with puberty and peer evaluations. At the same time, along with the onset of puberty comes a change in peer relationships. In addition to small same-sex dyads or cliques, adolescents increase their association with larger mixed-gender groups. Unfortunately, among young adolescents, negative interactions among peers in the form of sexual harassment, such as sexual comments, touching, or grabbing, increase (McMaster, Connolly, Pepler, & Craig, 2002). In particular, perpetration and experience of cross-gender sexual harassment increases over the middle school years for both girls and boys. Notably, cross-gender harassment was higher for young adolescents who were more advanced in their pubertal development. These findings provide support for our contention that peers respond to the social stimulus value of puberty, especially as an indicator that someone is now a sexual being. At the same time, young adolescents are beginning to pair up with other-gender peers to form some of their earliest romantic relationships. As teens mature into mid- and late adolescence, they begin to place greater importance on romantic relationships and in turn exhibit a shift in time spent with friends to time spent with romantic partners (Zimmer-Gembeck, 1999).

Romantic Relationships, Emotional Adjustment, and Puberty. Romantic relationships are important developmental contexts that shape girls' self-appraisals and adjustment. Whereas young adolescent girls strongly endorse the notion that it is desirable to be in love and have a romantic relationship (Simon, Eder, & Evans, 1992), regulating strong emotions experienced in relationships appears to take its toll on adolescent girls. For example, Joyner and Udry (2000) reported that involvement in romantic relationships was associated with higher depressive symptoms among adolescents who had a greater number of relationships over time, and among younger adolescents. Having more relationships indicates that youth were dealing with more breakups in relationships as well as negotiating new relationships. Breakups have been identified as a precursor of depressive episodes among adolescents (see Graber, 2004, for a review). In addition, younger adolescents may be more overwhelmed by the emotional strain of relationships. They have less experience in nondating social interactions that might have helped them prepare for subsequent challenges of regulating feelings and behaviors in dating situations. As noted, early maturers are more likely to engage in dating at younger ages (Ellis, 2004). In fact, Cauffman and Steinberg (1996) have found that early-maturing girls who dated at an early age were at risk for adjustment problems—in this case, increased eating pathology.

Initial romantic relationships and changes in adjustment are closely connected among girls in comparison to boys. In particular, gender differences in relationship goals, with girls being more likely than boys to focus on intimacy, make it particularly challenging for young adolescents to have relationships that meet their needs (Maccoby, 1998). Rudolf (2002) has suggested that girls experience greater stress than do boys in their interpersonal relationships and may internalize their experiences with peers to a greater extent. Thus, a particular challenge for girls is to find relationships that meet emotional needs along with interests in sexual activity.

As adolescent girls enter the dating world and begin to explore desires aroused by an interest in boys, many girls are often drawn to older and physically more mature males. This tendency to want and have older boyfriends can be quite risky for girls. For example, having an older boyfriend has been found to be a pathway to a range of problem behaviors among girls, such as early sexual activity, drinking, drug use, delinquency, and difficulty in school (Young & D'Arcy, 2005). Of note, given our focus on puberty, early maturation is a risk factor association with older peers—in particular, boys. Stattin and Magnusson (1990) were perhaps the first to report that association with older peers was linked to engagement in problem behaviors among early-maturing girls. As we have indicated, early-maturing girls who are dating are also more likely to report adjustment problems (Cauffman & Steinberg, 1996). In addition, among middle school students, Marín, Coyle, Gómez, Carvajal, and Kirby (2000) found that girls with older boyfriends had more unwanted sexual advances, had more friends who were sexually active, and were more likely to have had intercourse than other girls. Of note, these girls were also more likely to be earlier maturers. Of course, because early-maturing girls look older than their same-age peers, they are more likely to attract the attention of older boys.

NEW DIRECTIONS FOR CHILD AND ADOLESCENT DEVELOPMENT • DOI: 10.1002/cad

Romantic Relationships and Positive Sexual Development. We have previously suggested that one of the important gaps in the literature is understanding why older partners select younger, usually early-maturing girls (Graber et al., 1998, 1999). Are they in fact seeking a girl with less experience with boys who may therefore be an "easier" target? Are they rejected by their own same-age peers and hence seeking younger girls who may admire them? Earlier maturation puts girls at risk for involvement with older peers who are likely to be engaging in problem behaviors and places girls in situations for which they are less prepared because they have less experience with managing emerging sexual feelings. Older partners are likely a risk for any adolescent, but this experience more often occurs for some subgroups of girls.

In general, younger girls do not seem to manage the challenges of romantic relationships. Stricter regulation of relationships may be beneficial for younger girls. Such statements are clearly simplistic in that girls play an active role in desiring and forming romantic relationships. Girls' own self-evaluations about their bodies, their maturity, or other factors likely lead them to desire these partners. At the same time, it would be useful to examine in more depth what characterizes girls who develop more intimate relationships later rather than earlier in adolescence, for example, at ages sixteen or seventeen rather than thirteen or fourteen. This information would be useful in assisting parents and other adults in structuring the experiences of girls so that protective factors are enhanced. Once a girl has met and fallen for an older boy who drinks, uses drugs, or expects to have sex, it is much less likely that parents are going to be successful in stopping the relationship. Promoting involvement in activities that avoid association with deviant peers may be a better first step. We have also found that parental monitoring of behavior (knowing where adolescents are and who they are with) both enhances positive development and protects against risk among young adolescents (Graber et al., in press). Hence, parents should be reassured that their behaviors do make a difference for adolescent outcomes.

Puberty, Self, Peers, and Sexuality

In the course of this discussion, we have considered developmental changes in self and peer relationships that are associated with pubertal changes. Our final goal is to consider how these factors are connected more directly with sexuality and sexual behaviors.

To date, few studies have directly examined links between body image and sexuality. Rather, Buzwell and Rosenthal (1996) considered body image as an aspect of sexual identity, and sexual identity was linked to sexual behaviors. In this study, adolescents characterized by an overall sense of comfort with their sexual attitudes and behaviors (with positive self-appraisals), high efficacy about their abilities to regulate behaviors, and moderate to high value placed on commitment in sexual relationships usually engaged in healthy behaviors. Specifically, these adolescents tended to be fairly conscientious about avoiding risky behavior in sexual situations with casual partners but were less conscientious in situations with a regular partner, that is, someone with whom they had a reasonably stable relationship. Notably, this may be one of the only studies to consider positive self-development in connection with sexual behavior among adolescents.

Recently, Wingood, DiClemente, Harrington, and Davies (2002) found that poorer body image was associated with fear of abandonment and low rates of condom use during intercourse among African American girls. Poor body image was also associated with engaging in casual sex (Crosby et al., 2001). Wingood and colleagues (2002) note that these girls felt that they had fewer options for sexual partners and hence were less likely to engage in behaviors that might threaten relationships, like making requests or insisting on condom use. Hence, poor body image appears to be linked to aspects of one's sexual self like efficacy in sexual situations. It is interesting that the limited work on this issue focuses on African American girls, as it has generally been found that this group is more protected from body dissatisfaction in comparison to Caucasian girls (Parker et al., 1995). These findings indicate that body dissatisfaction may be expanding to more groups of adolescents and suggest that the impact of body dissatisfaction on sexuality merits investigation in all groups of adolescent girls.

The hypothesis that emotional adjustment is predictive of sexual behaviors has had some support. For example, Kessler and colleagues (1997), in a nationally representative survey, found that a history of affective, addictive, and conduct disorders was predictive of becoming a teen parent among women. Additional analyses revealed that this association was linked to sexual activity (that is, number of sexual partners) rather than consistency of contraception use. Interestingly, similar results were found among males in this study. In a study of adolescents, depressive symptoms were predictive of sexually transmitted diseases over time (Shrier, Harris, & Beardslee, 2002). Shrier and her colleagues suggest that adjustment problems may be predictive of sexual risk because adjustment problems and sexual risks share common correlates or predictors: poor impulse control, substance use, and poor social relationships.

One hypothesis from such findings is that sexual activity may be used to regulate negative mood. However, Fortenberry, Temkit, and Tu (2005) noted that sexual behavior is usually linked with positive moods and arousal rather than depression among adult women. Using a diary study with adolescent girls, they found that decreased levels of negative mood as well as partner support were associated with having intercourse. In some cases, sexual activity has been found to increase rather than decrease depressive moods among adolescent girls and young adult women depending on the context of the sexual experience, that is, whether the women hold particular values regarding sex and whether they engaged in sex in a relationship versus with a casual partner (Grello, Welsh, Harper, & Dickson, 2003).

NEW DIRECTIONS FOR CHILD AND ADOLESCENT DEVELOPMENT • DOI: 10.1002/cad

These studies do not draw a simple picture of positive adjustment resulting in healthy sexuality as demonstrated in healthy behaviors, or poor adjustment resulting in unhealthy sexuality. Rather, it may be that adolescent sexual experiences result in emotional consequences that require regulation and reappraisals of the self as adolescents reflect on their actions. In some cases, sexual experiences may lead to positive appraisals, with girls feeling that they had regulated their behavior in line with their beliefs and desires, had pleasurable experiences, or had experiences that brought them closer to a partner. In contrast, sexual experiences may not be evaluated positively and may result in negative feelings about oneself and one's sexuality.

As we have indicated, self-appraisals and puberty occur in a social context, in particular, in romantic relationships. The emotional costs of relationships may in part be due to the challenges of managing sexual feelings, as well as intimacy or even the interplay of both. Adolescent girls may be more upset about the breakup of a romantic relationship if the relationship also included greater expressions of sexual intimacy such as intercourse. It may be difficult to disentangle these issues in that the romantic relationships of adolescents are increasingly likely to include intercourse the longer the relationship lasts (Bearman, 2001); longer relationships may produce greater emotional stress if they dissolve. Also, girls who have intercourse at younger ages are thought to be at greater risk for a number of sexual health–related problems and are more likely to move on to a new sexual partner more quickly than older girls; that is, these girls are having more relationships (see Graber et al., 1999, for a review). In addition, poorly regulated sexual behavior, as seen in cases of infidelity, may be the source of problems in the relationship (Feldman & Cauffman, 1999). Many adolescents experience strong negative emotions such as sadness, despondency, and disillusionment in response to infidelities in romantic and sexual relationships (Feldman & Cauffman, 1999; Thompson, 1994).

Again, it is important to highlight that many of the challenges of emerging sexuality and relationships are normative developmental experiences, and most youth learn to regulate the emotional demands of relationships. We have already identified issues salient to more effective management of romantic relationships, and these factors extend to relationships that include intercourse and other sexual behaviors. Negative self-appraisals and poorer adjustment may play a role in riskier sexual behavior and the interplay of sex and relationships. Hence, intervening on these factors earlier in development may change the sexual trajectories for some girls.

Conclusion

In this discussion of puberty and sexuality, we have at times extended far from the actual experience of puberty, instead focusing on events and experiences that may be set in motion or altered by this experience. Puberty can be conceptualized as a developmental transition that has the potential to alter the course of developmental trajectories of adolescent behavior (Graber et al., 1998). How that transition is navigated depends on multiple factors. We have presented a few factors that we think are particularly salient to understanding what sets girls onto different trajectories during puberty. Much of the discussion of self, especially in terms of body image and adjustment, has focused on problems that girls experience. Because most girls move through puberty and adolescence without experiencing serious problems, the focus is on the subset of girls for whom puberty and the subsequent experiences of adolescence result in potentially lifelong difficulties in adjustment, relationships, and sexuality (Graber et al., 2004).

Our discussion has also been heterocentric, focusing on girls' emerging interests in boys. Given the heterocentric nature of the society that girls grow up in, it may be that all girls are exposed to pressure surrounding body image, appearance, and other- and same-gender peer acceptance. Less adherence to these norms would probably lead to healthier evaluations of one's sexuality for all girls. A fuller understanding of the impact of puberty, self-evaluations, and peers among different subgroups of girls is needed with a focus on a range of potential subgroups: girls who are more and less heterocentric in their developmental path, racial or ethnic subgroups of girls, girls who differ in maturational timing, and girls who have romantic relationships at younger versus older ages.

One of the unique issues of adolescence is that youth, even those who will likely traverse this decade of life with minimal difficulties, still seem to make unhealthy choices about sexual behaviors. Our hypothesis is that the development of sexuality as part of one's self-definition may play a critical role in these choices and that puberty, self, and peers are all essential components for how this develops. At the same time, we have identified many gaps in what is known about this developmental process and, moreover, how it links to behaviors. Sexuality is a normative part of development. Despite the societal interests in controlling sexual behaviors among youth, there seems to be little interest in figuring out how to help girls and their parents promote healthy views of their sexuality, including their self-appraisals, efficacy in regulating behaviors, and making connections with partners who meet girls' desires for emerging sexuality while maintaining health. Yet coming to terms with girls' sexuality and figuring out why some girls are successful in navigating the challenges of the social experience of puberty might be an informative method for identifying how to help girls enter healthy trajectories.

References

Alan Guttmacher Institute. (2001). *Teenage sexual and reproductive behavior in developed countries: Can more progress be made? Executive summary*. New York: Author.
Allgood-Merten, B., Lewinsohn, P. M., & Hops, H. (1990). Sex differences and adolescent depression. *Journal of Abnormal Psychology, 99*, 55–63.

Archibald, A. B., Graber, J. A., & Brooks-Gunn, J. (1999). Associations among parent-adolescent relationships, pubertal growth, dieting and body image in young adolescent girls: A short term longitudinal study. *Journal of Research on Adolescence, 9,* 395–415.

Bearman, P. (2001). *Middle school age youth: What do we know about sexual attitudes and behaviors of the under-15 set?* Paper presented at the National Campaign to Prevent Teen Pregnancy conference, New York.

Brooks-Gunn, J., Graber, J. A., & Paikoff, R. L. (1994). Studying links between hormones and negative affect: Models and measures. *Journal of Research on Adolescence, 4,* 469–486.

Brooks-Gunn, J., Petersen, A. C., & Eichorn, D. (1985). The study of maturational timing effects in adolescence. *Journal of Youth and Adolescence, 14,* 149–161.

Buzwell, S., & Rosenthal, D. (1996). Constructing a sexual self: Adolescents' sexual self-perceptions and sexual risk-taking. *Journal of Research on Adolescence, 6,* 489–513.

Cauffman, E., & Steinberg, L. (1996). Interactive effects of menarcheal status and dating on dieting and disordered eating among adolescent girls. *Developmental Psychology, 32,* 631–635.

Cavanagh, S. E. (2004). The sexual debut of girls in early adolescence: The intersection of race, pubertal timing, and friendship group characteristics. *Journal of Research on Adolescence, 14,* 285–312.

Compian, L., Gowen, L. K., & Hayward, C. (2004). Peripubertal girls' romantic and platonic involvement with boys: Associations with body image and depression symptoms. *Journal of Research on Adolescence, 14,* 23–47.

Crosby, R. A., DiClemente, R. J., Wingood, G. M., Sionean, C., Cobb, B. K., Harrington, K. F., Davies, S., Hook, E. W., & Oh, M. K. (2001). Correlates of casual sex among African-American female teens. *Journal of HIV/AIDS Prevention and Education for Adolescents and Children, 4,* 55–67.

Dohnt, H. K., & Tiggemann, M. (2004). Development of perceived body size and dieting awareness in young girls. *Perceptual and Motor Skills, 99,* 790–792.

Ellis, B. J. (2004). Timing of pubertal maturation in girls: An integrated life history approach. *Psychological Bulletin, 130,* 920–958.

Feldman, S. S., & Cauffman, E. (1999). Sexual betrayal among late adolescents: Perspectives of the perpetrator and the aggrieved. *Journal of Youth and Adolescence, 28,* 235–258.

Flannery, D. J., Rowe, D. C., & Gulley, B. L. (1993). Impact of pubertal status, timing, and age on adolescent sexual experience and delinquency. *Journal of Adolescent Research, 8,* 21–40.

Fortenberry, J. D., Temkit, M., & Tu, W. (2005). Daily mood, partner support, sexual interest, and sexual activity among adolescent women. *Health Psychology, 24,* 252–257.

Graber, J. A. (2003). Puberty in context. In C. Hayward (Ed.), *Gender differences at puberty* (pp. 307–325). Cambridge: Cambridge University Press.

Graber, J. A. (2004). Internalizing problems during adolescence. In R. M. Lerner & L. Steinberg (Eds.), *Handbook of adolescent psychology* (pp. 587–619). Hoboken, NJ: Wiley.

Graber, J. A., Britto, P. R., & Brooks-Gunn, J. (1999). What's love got to do with it? Adolescents' and young adults' beliefs about sexual and romantic relationships. In W. Furman, B. B. Brown, & C. Feiring (Eds.), *Contemporary perspectives on adolescent relationships* (pp. 364–395). Cambridge: Cambridge University Press.

Graber, J. A., Brooks-Gunn, J., & Galen, B. R. (1998). Betwixt and between: Sexuality in the context of adolescent transitions. In R. Jessor (Ed.), *New perspectives on adolescent risk behavior* (pp. 270–316). Cambridge: Cambridge University Press.

Graber, J. A., Nichols, T. R., Lynne, S. D., Brooks-Gunn, J., & Botvin, G. J. (in press). A longitudinal examination of family, friend, and media influences on competent versus risky behaviors among urban minority youth. *Applied Developmental Science.*

Graber, J. A., Petersen, A. C., & Brooks-Gunn, J. (1996). Pubertal processes: Methods, measures, and models. In J. A. Graber, J. Brooks-Gunn, & A. C. Petersen (Eds.), *Transitions through adolescence: Interpersonal domains and context* (pp. 23–53). Mahwah, NJ: Erlbaum.

Graber, J. A., Seeley, J. R., Brooks-Gunn, J., & Lewinsohn, P. M. (2004). Is pubertal timing associated with psychopathology in young adulthood? *Journal of the American Academy of Child and Adolescent Psychiatry, 43*(6), 718–726.

Grello, C. M., Welsh, D. P., Harper, M. S., & Dickson, J. W. (2003). Dating and sexual relationship trajectories and adolescent functioning. *Adolescent and Family Health, 3,* 103–112.

Grumbach, M. M., & Styne, D. M. (1998). Puberty: Ontogeny, neuroendocrinology, physiology, and disorders. In J. D. Wilson, D. W. Fostor, H. M. Kronenberg, & P. R. Larsen (Eds.), *Williams textbook of endocrinology* (pp. 1509–1625). Philadelphia: Saunders.

Halpern, C. T., Udry, J. R., Campbell, B., & Suchindran, C. (1999). Effects of body fat on weight concerns, dating, and sexual activity: A longitudinal analysis of Black and White adolescent girls. *Developmental Psychology, 35,* 721–736.

Herman-Giddens, M. E., Slora, E. J., Wasserman, R. C., Bourdony, C. J., Bhapkar, M. V., Koch, G. G., & Hasemeier, C. M. (1997). Secondary sexual characteristics and menses in young girls seen in office practice: A study of pediatric research in office settings network. *Pediatrics, 99,* 505–512.

Jones, D. C. (2004). Body image among adolescent girls and boys: A longitudinal study. *Developmental Psychology, 40,* 823–835.

Joyner, K., & Udry, J. R. (2000). You don't bring me anything but down: Adolescent romance and depression. *Journal of Health and Social Behavior, 41,* 369–391.

Kessler, R. C., Berglund, P. A., Foster, C. L., Saunders, W. B., Stang, P. E., & Walters, E. E. (1997). Social consequences of psychiatric disorders, II: Teenage parenthood. *American Journal of Psychiatry, 154,* 1405–1411.

Maccoby, E. E. (1998). *Two sexes: Growing up apart, coming together.* Cambridge, MA: Harvard University Press.

Marín, B. V., Coyle, K. K., Gómez, C. A., Carvajal, S. C., & Kirby, D. B. (2000). Older boyfriends and girlfriends increase risk of sexual initiation in young adolescents. *Journal of Adolescent Health, 27,* 409–418.

Masten, A. S., & Curtis, W. J. (2000). Integrating competence and psychopathology: Pathways toward a comprehensive science of adaptation in development. *Development and Psychopathology, 12,* 529–550.

McKenna, K. E. (2001). Neural circuitry involved in sexual function. *Journal of Spinal Cord Medicine, 24,* 148–154.

McMaster, L. E., Connolly, J., Pepler, D., & Craig, W. M. (2002). Peer to peer sexual harassment in early adolescence: A developmental perspective. *Development and Psychopathology, 14,* 91–105.

Ohring, R., Graber, J. A., & Brooks-Gunn, J. (2002). Girls' recurrent and concurrent body dissatisfaction: Correlates and consequences over eight years. *International Journal of Eating Disorders, 31,* 404–415.

Parker, S., Nichter, M., Nichter, M., Vuckovic, N., Sims, C., & Ritenbaugh, C. (1995). Body image and weight concerns among African-American and White adolescent females: Differences that make a difference. *Human Organization, 54,* 103–114.

Ricciardelli, L. A., McCabe, M. P., & Holt, K. E. (2003). A biopsychosocial model for understanding body image and body change strategies among children. *Journal of Applied Developmental Psychology, 24,* 475–495.

Rudolf, K. D. (2002). Gender differences in emotional responses to interpersonal stress during adolescence. *Journal of Adolescent Health, 30* (Suppl.), 3–13.

Shrier, L. A., Harris, S. K., & Beardslee, W. R. (2002). Temporal associations between depressive symptoms and self-reported sexually transmitted disease among adolescents. *Archives of Pediatrics and Adolescent Medicine, 156,* 599–606.

Simon, R. W., Eder, D., & Evans, C. (1992). The development of feeling norms underlying romantic love among adolescent females. *Social Psychology Quarterly, 55,* 29–46.

Stattin, H., & Magnusson, D. (1990). *Paths through life: Vol. 2. Pubertal maturation in female development.* Mahwah, NJ: Erlbaum.

Stice, E. (2003). Puberty and body image. In C. Hayward (Ed.), *Gender differences at puberty* (pp. 61–76). Cambridge: Cambridge University Press.

Tanner, J. M. (1962). *Growth at adolescence.* Cambridge, MA: Blackwell.

Thompson, S. (1994). Changing lives, changing genres: Teenage girls' narratives about sex and romance, 1978–1986. In A. S. Rossi (Ed.), *Sexuality across the life course* (pp. 209–232). Chicago: University of Chicago Press.

Udry, J. R., & Campbell, B. C. (1994). Getting started on sexual behavior. In A. S. Rossi (Ed.), *Sexuality across the life course* (pp. 187–207). Chicago: University of Chicago Press.

Williams, J. M., & Currie, C. (2000). Self-esteem and physical development in early adolescence: Pubertal timing and body image. *Journal of Early Adolescence, 20,* 129–149.

Wingood, G. M., DiClemente, R. J., Harrington, K., & Davies, S. (2002). Body image and African American females' sexual health. *Journal of Women's Health and Gender-Based Medicine, 11,* 433–439.

Young, A. M., & D'Arcy, H. (2005). Older boyfriends of adolescent girls: The cause or a sign of the problem? *Journal of Adolescent Health, 36,* 410–419.

Zimmer-Gembeck, M. J. (1999). Stability, change and individual differences in involvement with friends and romantic partners among adolescent females. *Journal of Youth and Adolescence, 28,* 419–438.

JULIA A. GRABER is associate professor of psychology at the University of Florida.

LISA M. SONTAG is a graduate student in developmental psychology at the University of Florida.

NEW DIRECTIONS FOR CHILD AND ADOLESCENT DEVELOPMENT • DOI: 10.1002/cad

4

This chapter provides an expanded view of parent-adolescent sexual communication and socialization in an effort to move beyond risk perspectives toward a consideration of other important aspects of sexual socialization.

Positive Sexual Communication and Socialization in the Parent-Adolescent Context

Eva S. Lefkowitz, Tara M. Stoppa

MOTHER: So when do you feel is a good time to date? For you?
DAUGHTER: For me? Just plain ol' dating?
MOTHER: Which means?
DAUGHTER: Just going out. Like to a movie . . . or like we go to a hangout and then go to a movie . . . or like we go to a movie and then to a hangout. . . . But if I'm getting into the major stuff, that'd be like laaaaater.
MOTHER: What's major stuff?
DAUGHTER: Don't make it hard on me! You know what I'm talking about!

In this example from an observational study (Lefkowitz, Boone, Sigman, & Au, 2002), a mother and her daughter discuss dating and sexuality. Within a few exchanges, they have referred to dating in a somewhat specific way, as well as referred to sexual behavior in a vaguer and more indirect way. The mother and daughter seem to be relatively open about this topic. However, the daughter does appear to be somewhat uncomfortable, and for both, their

We thank Terry Au, Tanya Boone, Rosalie Corona, Graciela Espinosa-Hernandez, Susan McHale, Laura Romo, Cindy Shearer, and Marian Sigman. Discussions with these collaborators over the years have helped us to develop some of the ideas in this chapter. Work on this chapter was supported by grants from the National Institutes of Health, NRSA MH 11225 and R-01 HD 41720.

use of vague terminology (for example, "major stuff") suggests some embarrassment. The process of communication appears to be at least as important as what is actually discussed. In fact, as much as two-thirds of communication may be conveyed through nonverbal channels (Burgoon, 1985). However, research on communication about sex-related topics has generally relied on examinations of verbal communication. Specifically, much research has examined the topics that parents (usually mothers) and offspring discuss. As a result, we now know a fair bit about the frequency with which mothers and adolescents engage in discussions of sex-related topics and have some, though more limited, knowledge about the specific topics that they discuss. We have much less information, however, about the process and quality of this communication. Moreover, the majority of this work relies predominantly on a risk perspective. In general, most researchers have examined how communication can protect adolescents from risky behaviors. However, messages that parents convey to their daughters about risk are only one part of the socialization that occurs around sexuality.

Parents are, in most cases, one of the earliest sources of socialization for positive sexual development. By adolescence, individuals likely also experience socialization from a number of other sources, including schools, media, and peers. Nevertheless, parents continue to play an important role here, providing unique messages and helping adolescents interpret messages from other sources.

In this chapter, we describe other ways that parents socialize their daughters' sexuality, including the influence of parental belief systems, the content of conversations, the style and process of communication, and indirect socialization. By focusing on the process and style of communication, we go beyond a risk perspective to consider the socialization of positive sexual development, highlighting parents' roles in this process. We also discuss the importance of developmentally appropriate communication and offer directions for future research. When possible, we provide relevant examples from the literature to support our ideas. We also offer examples of conversations between mothers and daughters from our own research. It is important to note that although we focus on parents and daughters, given the nature of this volume, we believe that many of these ideas apply to the socialization of sons' sexuality as well.

Parents' Belief Systems

One generally accepted idea about familial socialization is that parents' belief systems influence the development of their children's belief systems. Although little research has examined this issue, we believe it is important to understand parents' beliefs about sexuality in order to understand the process of family socialization around sexuality. The effectiveness of sex-related communication may depend on parents' own values and attitudes (Moore, Peterson, & Furstenberg, 1986). Some parents may take a risk-prevention perspective, either teaching their daughters to avoid the dangers of sexual encounters altogether or encouraging them to protect themselves (for example, by using condoms or birth control pills) from negative outcomes such as sexually transmitted diseases (STDs) or pregnancy. Other parents may focus more generally on teaching their daughters about sexuality. Avoiding dangers may be part of this communication but is not the predominant aspect. There is often an assumption that parents are more conservative in their beliefs than their children are, but this is not necessarily always the case. Consider this conversation between a mother and her twelve-year-old daughter:

MOTHER: What about sex?
DAUGHTER: Don't do it 'til you're married!
MOTHER: Who says that?
DAUGHTER: Me!
MOTHER: Oh really?
DAUGHTER: Yeah . . . when you get married . . . after college.
MOTHER: Well, I don't personally think you have to wait until you're married . . . but you should be in love with someone. . . . That's just my opinion.

Here, the mother explains to her daughter that her criterion for sex is to be in love. Thus, parents' messages about sex are not always prohibitive.

Another aspect of parents' beliefs is what they want their children to learn. We would imagine that parents almost never want their child to get an STD or become unintentionally pregnant. However, an individual's belief system inevitably influences how he or she conveys these messages and what behaviors this person describes as appropriate. Some parents believe in abstinence until marriage, and they want to convey this belief system to their children. Other parents may believe that sexual activity in the context of a committed relationship is acceptable if safe, or that their child should wait until a certain age, but not necessarily until marriage.

Although not a belief system, parents' own comfort with sexuality can be an important determinant of their ability to socialize their children. It is unlikely that many parents feel extremely comfortable and at ease talking to their daughters about sex. However, some parents may feel more or less comfortable than others based on their own life experiences. Thus, this level of comfort can bear on how often parents talk about sex-related issues as well as the manner in which they discuss them. Beyond belief systems and communication comfort, we rarely think about parents' sexuality when examining parent-child communication about sex. It is likely, though, that parents' own healthy sexual development influences their ability to socialize their daughters. Parents who have not developed a clear sense of sexual self are unlikely to be successful at helping their daughters in their own development.

Content of Sex-Related Communication

Much work to date has focused on parents' discussions with their children about sex-related risks. Some of the most frequently discussed topics between mothers and adolescents are STDs and AIDS, dating and sexual behavior, pregnancy, abstinence, and menstruation (DiIorio, Kelley, & Hockenberry-Eaton, 1999; Lefkowitz & Espinosa-Hernandez, 2005; Rosenthal & Feldman, 1999).

Although some existing work has demonstrated links between the frequency of sex-related communication and sexual behaviors, these associations are not always in predicted directions (Fox & Inazu, 1980; Jaccard, Dittus, & Gordon, 1996; Lefkowitz & Espinosa-Hernandez, 2005). More recently, researchers have used more complex measures of sex-related communication that examine multiple topics of discussion, collect information from both offspring and mothers, and use more precise scales. As measures have become more sophisticated, researchers have improved their ability to find such associations. For instance, more extensive sex-related communication has been shown to be associated with reduced frequency of intercourse and unprotected sex (Hutchinson, Jemmott, Jemmott, Braverman, & Fong, 2003; Kotva & Schneider, 1990).

Sexual socialization spans a larger range of topics than those traditionally examined. In fact, in our own observational work, when asked to talk about "dating and sexuality," mothers and adolescents spent about 40 percent of conversations talking about dating, 17 percent talking about sex, and 38 percent off topic (Lefkowitz et al., 2002). However, topics coded "off topic" may have also been tangentially relevant to sex-related communication. For example, mothers and offspring sometimes engaged in metacommunication about sex, for instance, talking about whether a daughter had learned about sex in health class. Other mother-offspring pairs ended up off topic through the natural flow of conversation, for example, by first discussing when the child might be old enough to start dating, but then naturally moving to a discussion of growing up more generally (Lefkowitz et al., 2002).

Within the context of discussing dating, parents and daughters could cover a range of topics. Parents may see discussing dating as a safer way of bringing up sex-related issues. They can talk about their views on relationships without being direct about sexual topics. For instance, after a thirteen-year-old daughter told her mother she thought sixteen was a good age to start dating, the mother asked some follow-up questions:

MOTHER: What are your expectations? . . . What do you think you should be able to do when you say *date*?
DAUGHTER: Go to the movies.
MOTHER: What time of day should you be able to do these things?
DAUGHTER: In the evening.
MOTHER: You can go to the library together. . . . You may think that's boring, but you can go to museums. . . . Going on a date doesn't always have

to be in the evening. Going on a date means doing something fun. You can learn, do something productive. It can be a productive experience. . . . That's what you should be thinking when you go on a date.

This mother explicitly discusses dating with her daughter, but there is also an undertone of avoiding risky situations or getting too serious.

In addition to relationships and sexual behavior, we believe that sexual socialization includes a much broader range of communication. Particularly with younger adolescents, parents often talk to their daughters about physical development, puberty, and menstruation (Baumeister, Flores, & Marin, 1995; DiIorio et al., 1999; Raffaelli et al., 1999; Rosenthal & Feldman, 1999). Although much work has focused on sexual intercourse, sexuality communication is also likely to include other sexual behaviors, such as solitary sex (for instance, masturbation or wet dreams; DiIorio et al., 1999; Rosenthal & Feldman, 1999), kissing and making out, and oral sex. Holding hands and other affectionate gestures could be discussed within this context. Just as certain sexual behaviors are considered gateways to sexual intercourse (Feldman, Turner, & Araujo, 1999), so might talking about certain behaviors be gateways to talking about intercourse. For instance, one mother and daughter in our study had the following exchange:

DAUGHTER: But right now, in middle school, going out, is just basically, you're boyfriend and girlfriend, and then like, I guess you kiss.
MOTHER: Yes.
DAUGHTER: It's not that big a deal.
MOTHER: What kind of kissing?
DAUGHTER: Well, a little tongue action there but [*mother gives daughter a stern look*], Mom, I've done it before, it's not, like, that bad.
MOTHER: Well, that was, like, spin the bottle, but I mean, that's the kind of thing, that it starts, to lead to other things. . . .
DAUGHTER: Yes, but I won't go far, because I'm too, like, I won't, I believe . . .
MOTHER: What's going far?
DAUGHTER: Well, the farthest I'll go, just to put it that way, is kissing.
MOTHER: Mm hum.
DAUGHTER: Kissing, like really kissing, not just a peck.
MOTHER: Mm hum, what about when a boy starts trying to touch your breasts?
DAUGHTER: I don't have any [*laughing*] so no boys would!

This dyad is able to talk about kissing, but within the framework of gateway behaviors.

Sexual socialization may also include messages about sexual orientation and sexual identity. In general, work with high school students suggests that about 70 percent of daughters report discussing homosexuality (for example,

NEW DIRECTIONS FOR CHILD AND ADOLESCENT DEVELOPMENT • DOI: 10.1002/cad

gay and lesbian issues) with their mothers, and about 60 percent report having discussed these issues with their fathers (Rosenthal & Feldman, 1999). Most of the research that examines communication about sexual orientation, however, focuses on disclosure of sexual orientation to parents (D'Augelli, Hershberger, & Pilkington, 1998; Hillier, 2002; Savin-Williams & Dubé, 1998). Work in this area suggests that many sexual-minority daughters do talk to their parents about their sexual orientation, with reactions ranging from full acceptance to rejection (D'Augelli et al., 1998).

Sexual orientation may also be discussed in a number of other contexts. Parents and daughters may talk about someone they know who is gay, lesbian, or bisexual and through this conversation convey their own (dis)approval. In our work, when we asked mothers and offspring to discuss "dating and sexuality," some offspring thought that by "sexuality," we were referring to sexual orientation, and mothers used this opportunity to discuss the distinction between sexuality in general and sexual orientation or preference. For example, in the following conversation, a mother introduces the concept of sexual preference with her daughter:

MOTHER: *Sexuality.* What do you think it means?
DAUGHTER: When you have sex.
MOTHER: Basically. But it's a little more than that.
DAUGHTER: When you have kids.
MOTHER: What are you attracted to . . . males or females?
DAUGHTER: Males! I'm straight!
MOTHER: Some people are attracted to both. Or some people are attracted to one or the other.

This mother appears to present the topic in a nonjudgmental way, letting her child know sexual orientation is a normative part of development. Other parents might send less positive messages to their offspring about sexual-minority individuals, whether or not their offspring are themselves heterosexual.

Parents and adolescents may also discuss the moral or religious aspects of sexuality. Research suggests that parents and offspring often discuss topics such as whether premarital sex is okay (Raffaelli et al., 1999), regretting not waiting until marriage (Jaccard, Dittus, & Gordon, 1998), or general moral aspects of sexuality (Raffaelli & Ontai, 2001). Although it may be more challenging to quantify these types of conversations compared to conversations about dating or abstinence, we have seen evidence for such conversations in our own work. For instance, one mother said to her eleven-year-old daughter:

MOTHER: You know, the church won't allow that [intercourse before marriage]. You want to give yourself to Jesus . . . as his bride . . . until you meet a man and you get married and you know that he's the right person for you and he's going to make you happy for the rest of your life. Sex before marriage is not right [*shakes head*].
DAUGHTER: I know. Believe me! I know!

What is moral may be a bit unclear in other cases. In other examples from this work, we found that mothers and adolescents commonly discussed waiting until the child was older to have sex (Lefkowitz, Boone, Au, & Sigman, 2003). That is, the mothers were not necessarily suggesting waiting until marriage, but they were encouraging postponing sex until a—sometimes unspecified—future time. For instance, one mother said to her daughter, "Well, actually, you know, the truth is, I don't think you have to wait until you get married, but I think you should be in love with someone first, maybe like in college or something, that's just what I think." On a self-report measure, this family might not have said that they discussed morality, but this discussion is indicative of the mother's moral belief system. Parents have to balance the desire for their children to develop their own moral sensibilities with a desire to provide moral guidance and direction. We believe that it is important for parents to talk to their children about their own moral perspective. Jaccard et al. (1998) found that adolescents underestimated the extent to which mothers disapproved of their child's becoming sexually active, suggesting that mothers may not sufficiently communicate their own moral perspective. Adolescent girls are likely to hear about morality from many different sources: school, media, friends, religious institutions, and even politicians. Therefore, parents should consider discussing their own moral perspectives as adolescents work to incorporate these different views into their own worldview.

Do parents talk to their children about sexual desire, sexual pleasure, and even orgasm? Researchers have not frequently asked about these topics. When they have, they have found that these topics are infrequently discussed. Rosenthal and Feldman (1999) found that 94 percent of high school girls had never discussed sexual desire with their fathers, and 76 percent had never discussed desire with their mothers. In our work, we asked first-semester college students how much they had discussed a number of sex-related topics with their mothers in the past three months (Lefkowitz & Espinosa-Hernandez, 2006). On average, sexual desire and sexual satisfaction were discussed very infrequently with mothers (less than once). However, a minority of students reported having discussed sexual desire or satisfaction a few times or often, demonstrating individual variation in addressing these topics. To fully understand sexual socialization, it is necessary that we understand how parents socialize their daughters to be sexual beings, not only by examining what parents prohibit but also learning what parents teach daughters about the pleasurable aspects of sexuality.

Although discussing explicit topics such as sexual desire may be difficult between parents and daughters, they may also broach these topics by discussing more socially acceptable themes. For instance, mothers and daughters, in particular, may discuss physical attractiveness. Although we know of few data on this topic, in our first-semester college sample described above, only 32 percent reported that they had not discussed the physical attractiveness of the opposite sex with their mothers in the past three months (Lefkowitz & Espinosa-Hernandez, 2006). It is likely that girls

NEW DIRECTIONS FOR CHILD AND ADOLESCENT DEVELOPMENT • DOI: 10.1002/cad

and their mothers discuss cute boys and attractive celebrities, or that mothers are present when these conversations happen with friends. These topics may be a safe way for mothers and daughters to discuss attraction and desire without talking about sex. It will be important, in future research, to examine these types of conversations between parents and adolescents as another possible gateway into discussing sexuality.

The range of topics that parents may discuss with their children is large and far reaching. Although all families are different, we believe that over time, parents are most likely to help socialize their daughters for positive sexual development by discussing a large range of topics: risk and preventive measures, of course, but also physical development, romantic relationships, desire, sexual identity and orientation, and moral aspects of sexuality.

Style and Process of Communication

In our past work, we have stressed the importance of examining not only the content of communication but also how sexual information is conveyed, including the quality of communication (Lefkowitz et al., 2002; Lefkowitz, Romo, Corona, Au, & Sigman, 2000; Lefkowitz, Kahlbaugh, & Sigman, 1996). Having a positive relationship and high-quality general communication are likely to be necessary, but not sufficient, conditions for having positive sex-related communication. That is, parents and offspring who have poor relationships and difficulty communicating about everyday issues are unlikely to have great sex-related communication. However, families with good relationships and positive general communication may or may not have positive sex-related communication. Thus, understanding girls' positive sexual development in the context of the parent-offspring relationship involves understanding the family context more generally.

Specific to sex-related communication, researchers have found links between the quality of sex-related communication and sexual behaviors (East, 1996; Handelsman, Cabral, & Weisfeld, 1987; Lefkowitz & Espinosa-Hernandez, 2006). For instance, Guzman et al. (2003) reported that Latino adolescents who are more comfortable talking to their parents about sex-related topics are less likely to be sexually active and tend to have a later age of first intercourse. Communication may also be important once adolescents become sexually active. Handelsman et al. (1987) found that among sexually active high school students, students who used birth control reported better-quality communication than students who did not.

We have examined quality of communication through both self-report and observational methods. In our self-report work, we have asked adolescents or emerging adults to describe the level of comfort and openness in their sex-related communication with their mothers (Lefkowitz & Espinosa-Hernandez, 2006). Students reported feeling more open and comfortable discussing sex-related topics with their close friends than with their mothers, although those who felt more comfortable talking to mothers also felt more comfortable talking to friends. Better-quality communication with mothers was associated with more positive beliefs about condoms and self-efficacy for using condoms.

In our observational work, we have examined various aspects of sex-related communication, including the extent to which mothers dominate conversations about sex (Lefkowitz et al., 2000), turn taking during sex-related conversations (Lefkowitz et al., 1996), and positive and negative affective style (Lefkowitz, Sigman, & Au, 2002). Findings suggest that conversations about sexuality involved less turn taking and fewer words than other mother-child conversations (Lefkowitz et al., 1996). Mothers and daughters, more so than mothers and sons, demonstrated mutuality of affect, with significant associations between mothers' positive behaviors and daughters' positive and negative behaviors during sex-related conversations (Lefkowitz et al., 2002).

Parents also convey a great deal about their beliefs and feelings through not only what they say and how they say it, but what they do not say. By appearing extremely uncomfortable or unable to discuss sex-related topics, parents send a message to their daughters that sex is difficult to discuss, secretive, or dirty. Consider, for instance, this conversation between a mother and her daughter:

MOTHER: Safe sex? Wow! [*looks uncomfortable*] Okay. Maybe I'm going to go to the library and get you a book . . . let you read it to understand. [*pause*] Okay, you want to tell me that nobody in your classroom talked to you about that? [*daughter shakes head no*] I was your age and I know kids are always talking [*hand-gestures talking motions*] . . . gossiping.
DAUGHTER: No, we never gossip. . . . Never!
MOTHER: Well, then, if nobody gossips, then I'm going to go to the library and get you some books to help you understand and we'll talk about it . . . some very simple books to help you understand about sex.

Here the mother conveys to her daughter that she is uncomfortable talking about sex and that it would be easier if her daughter read about it in a book. This example provides evidence that communication is not always direct. Parents may avoid communication or may outsource such conversations by asking someone else to talk to their daughters about sexuality, such as a friend or sibling of the parent. Parents may also provide daughters with written literature about sexuality rather than talking directly to them. Fathers may be indirect socializers of sexuality more often than not. That is, fathers are less likely than mothers to talk about sexuality (Fisher, 1986; Rosenthal & Feldman, 1999), but it is likely that fathers socialize daughters in other ways. Jokes about sexuality that are not overtly "birds and bees" talks provide powerful messages to daughters. A father may joke that his daughters are going to be locked in their room until they are twenty-one years old so that they do not begin to date. Although not explicitly a conversation about sex, such jokes provide daughters with information about their father's views about romance and dating.

Moreover, our observational work suggests that mothers tend to dominate conversations about sexuality more than they do conversations about other topics such as everyday or conflict issues (Lefkowitz et al., 1996). There appears to be a tendency to take on more of a lecturing-teaching role when discussing sexuality. This didactic approach may be due to mothers' own discomfort when discussing these topics (Rosenthal & Feldman, 1999). In addition, mothers may feel that conveying this information is extremely important. If they do not convey their point during a disagreement about everyday issues, the worst consequences might be a messy room. In contrast, sexuality conversations have very important implications, such as unwanted pregnancy and sexually transmitted diseases.

Research on learning and memory, however, suggests that lecturing is a less effective style for learning than are more interactive discussions (Jacoby, 1978). We have found that mothers often use either yes-no questions when the correct answer is obvious (for example, "Can you get AIDS from having unprotected sex?"), or even worse, the "did ya know?" question, where the child merely needs to say yes to avoid spending more time on the embarrassing topic (for example, "Did ya know that using condoms can prevent AIDS?"). To this end, in our intervention work we have encouraged mothers to master the use of open-ended questions (Lefkowitz et al., 2000).

By using open-ended questions, mothers can probe their adolescent's existing knowledge and belief systems. For instance, in this example (with a son), the mother probes her child's incorrect responses to discover what he does and does not know:

MOTHER: How do you not get AIDS?
SON: You just don't, you don't share needles, or nothing like that, you protect yourself when you are having sex.
MOTHER: And how do you protect yourself when you're having sex?
SON: Well, you can use, there's like so much stuff, you can use birth pill for women, you can use foam, use a condom for women, you could use a condom for guys.
MOTHER: Will, will foam and birth control pills protect you from AIDS?
SON: They say they will, I don't know if they will.
MOTHER: Absolutely not, listen . . . when you start having sex, [you] had better use a latex condom, okay?

Contrast this open-ended question approach with the following:

MOTHER: The thing is, if you really fall in love with somebody—you know, like Romeo and Juliet—you really love somebody and you want to be with them, it's something you should really talk about. And if it's something that you are ready to do and you want to do, and you do it because you want to do it, not because you feel pressured into doing it, then you should think about birth control. And always feel like you can talk to me, and if you don't want to talk to me, that you can talk to an adult who understands. *[daughter nods affirmatively]* You know, because [your grandparents] made me feel really bad about it. To them, it was forbidden. And I was so scared. And I don't think that was good.

Although in this conversation, the message seems supportive, kind, and flexible, it is never clear the extent to which the daughter is listening, what the daughter's own belief system is, or what the daughter knows about intercourse or birth control. We are not suggesting that mothers should never convey their own opinions or express their own beliefs to their daughters. Instead, we are highlighting the importance of including interactive conversations and open-ended questions when discussing sex-related topics. We are also attempting to show how two conversations conveying the same beliefs and content could have strikingly different results, depending on the way the message is conveyed.

In addition to the content and quality of sexual communication, the context is important. When do parents talk to their daughters about sex-related topics? Although the traditional image of a sex talk is a formal discussion of the "birds and bees," it is likely that many of these conversations happen in the context of daily lives. In our observational research, one mother-daughter pair asked to move their chairs to face forward and switched positions so that they could mimic their most common context for having serious conversations—in the car. Parents may also take advantage of naturally occurring events, such as learning that a daughter's best friend has a date or the content in a television program watched jointly, to discuss sex-related topics. However, because much research assumes a planned and purposeful nature to such conversations, we know very little about these contexts. In addition, we know very little about who else is present during these conversations. Do parents discuss these topics jointly or separately? Are they discussed with multiple siblings at once or separately?

Although families are diverse and there is no one right way to socialize daughters around sexuality, we do believe there are better and worse communication processes. Ideally, parents should provide an environment that is open and comfortable for these discussions. They should seize opportune moments to discuss sex-related topics, which may be less awkward and more natural than a formal discussion about sex. Parents should try to engage daughters in these conversations, asking questions and probing their daughters for their own knowledge and beliefs. The more positive and less negative affect involved, the more likely parents are to engage their daughters.

NEW DIRECTIONS FOR CHILD AND ADOLESCENT DEVELOPMENT • DOI: 10.1002/cad

Indirect Socialization

Modeling is likely to play an important role in the area of sexual socialization. Modeling may be particularly salient in families where parents are single, dating, or remarried. A child of a parent who is dating is confronted with that parent's sexuality, often on a daily basis. The parent's sexuality may become a topic of discussion, or the child may see the parent interact with romantic partners. Parents who appear to be comfortable with their own sexuality may convey a message that sexuality is natural, whereas parents who feel more discomfort in this area may communicate that sexuality should be hidden or is shameful. Parents may also use their own experiences to discuss the child's dating or sexuality, as this mother does:

MOTHER: So where do you think sex is? Is it involved in dating?
DAUGHTER: After the marriage. Or maybe after the sixth or seventh date.
MOTHER: But what if you like this person as a friend and not like a boyfriend?
DAUGHTER: Well, then you say, "Let's just be friends."
MOTHER: Because I just want to be clear on that. Because I've gone out many, many times and I just wanna be friends . . . I mean I've gone out with [name] more than five times and I don't want to sleep with him.

Here the mother draws on her own experiences to discuss the idea that sexual involvement does not have to happen early in the sequence of dating. Of course, parents' own sexuality is important not only for single parents. How parents in committed partnerships display affection toward each other may also teach daughters about sexuality, romance, and love in powerful ways.

Modeling is only one way that parents can socialize their daughters without ever directly talking about sexuality. In some families, rules and standards for sons and daughters may differ. By allowing more dating and sexual freedom for sons than for daughters, parents may teach their children about gender roles in romance and sexuality and perpetuate a sexual double standard that continues to exist today (Crawford & Popp, 2003; Shearer, Hosterman, Gillen, & Lefkowitz, 2005).

Given the amount of sexuality present in music, print, television, and movies, parents' restrictions on media access will affect the messages their daughters receive. In experimental work, Ward, Hansbrough, and Walker (2005) demonstrated that exposing high school students to music videos with stereotypical content led to more traditional views about sexual relationships and gender, compared to those not exposed to such videos. In addition to limiting their daughters' media choices, parents can also help their daughters with media literacy. Parents who watch mature content with their daughters and discuss it with them afterward are sending different messages from parents who forbid these programs or parents who do not monitor their daughters' media diets.

NEW DIRECTIONS FOR CHILD AND ADOLESCENT DEVELOPMENT • DOI: 10.1002/cad

Developmentally Appropriate Communication

Although some research has investigated age differences in sexuality communication, little work has used a developmental model to do so. The findings on age differences have been mixed. Some researchers report that mothers talk with older adolescents about sex-related topics more than with younger adolescents (Lefkowitz et al., 2000; White, Wright, & Barnes, 1995). Other work reports no associations between age and frequency of sex-related communication (Fisher, 1986; Raffaelli, Bogenschneider, & Flood, 1998). These conflicting findings may be partly attributable to differences in the topics included in questionnaires. Mothers may find certain topics more appropriate for younger adolescents (puberty, for example) and others for older adolescents (safer sex). In our work, adolescents who discussed safer sex with their mothers were on average almost a year older than adolescents who did not (Lefkowitz et al., 2003). In contrast, we found no age differences based on whether mothers and adolescents had discussed abstinence. Thus, the number of topics mothers and their children report discussing may depend on what topics are listed in the questionnaires. It is therefore important to go beyond asking how many topics should be addressed and ask instead what topics should be discussed.

Chronological age may be less important than other developmental factors, such as pubertal development or sexual experience. A mother's discussion of condoms with a fourteen-year-old daughter who has never kissed another adolescent is likely to have different meaning from a similar discussion with a sexually active fourteen-year-old girl. In fact, Clawson and Reese-Weber (2003) reported that adolescents who experience conversations about sex-related topics before they become sexually active had a later age at first intercourse and fewer partners than those who have such conversations after first intercourse. However, they also found greater pregnancy rates in those who experienced on-time sexuality discussions, suggesting that these associations are complex and that more needs to be known about the timing of such conversations. It is likely that the better parents know their own daughters, the better able they will be to tailor a sex-related conversation to the experience, knowledge, and developmental stage of the adolescent.

Future Research Directions

Mostly, we have presented past work as though the findings were universal. However, evidence suggests that cultural background is an important determinant of topics discussed, communication style, and associations between communication and sexual behaviors. It is important to continue to develop an understanding of how communication about sex-related topics may differ depending on, for instance, race, socioeconomic status, country of origin, or religious background. Some girls from Latino backgrounds, for example, may experience more prohibition against dating and romantic interactions than girls from other backgrounds (Raffaelli & Ontai, 2001).

NEW DIRECTIONS FOR CHILD AND ADOLESCENT DEVELOPMENT • DOI: 10.1002/cad

The style of conversations between Latina American mothers and daughters also differs from conversations between European American mothers and daughters (Lefkowitz et al., 2000). Although there has been limited research on girls who are not Christian, evidence suggests that Muslim girls may experience very limited communication with their mothers about sex-related topics, and when they do have such conversations, they focus on risks to the individual and the social order (Orgocka, 2004).

Many of the areas explored in this chapter are also important directions for future research. In addition to developing measures of new and under-studied topics of sex-related communication, researchers should continue to examine facets of communication that go beyond content of conversations in order to develop an understanding of comfort, openness, and other aspects of communication quality. It will also be important to understand how the content and quality of communication uniquely explain variation in adolescents' sexual attitudes and behaviors. By sexual attitudes and behaviors, we mean not only risk behaviors, but also the broader development of a healthy sexual self, including sexual exploration and comfort with one's body. Moreover, future research should also seek to understand the context and developmental trajectory of sexual socialization.

Finally, we encourage researchers to continue to use methodologies that complement traditional survey methodology, such as observational techniques, interviews, ethnography, and diary methods. The few studies in this area that have used these types of methodologies have provided rich data that could not always be captured from questionnaires. These types of methodologies may be particularly important with understudied populations, so that research avoids preconceived notions.

We end this chapter with one final example from a mother-daughter conversation. We provide this example because we believe it demonstrates communication that is likely to foster positive sexual development. This mother and daughter discuss a range of topics, including dating and when teenagers are mature enough to have sex. The mother has established an open and comfortable environment for talking about sexuality. She asks questions, and both the mother and daughter are engaged in the discussion (even if the daughter does mock her mother a bit). Despite being mocked, the mother makes it clear that she wants to continue to have such conversations and establishes an environment receptive to future positive socialization interactions. The daughter is clearly engaged in the discussion and is listening to her mother despite her playfulness. The mother does not focus so much on the daughter's sexuality but talks more about a hypothetical teenager rather than asking the daughter at what age she should first have sex. It is likely that this conversation, captured in the lab, is a snippet of a much larger history of socialization around sexuality in this family. The hope is that the daughter's ability to be critical about her mother's views on sexuality will transfer to what she hears from other sources like the media or friends.

MOTHER: Sexuality . . . what are your feelings on that? [*pause*] I read recently that the average age teenagers have sex is sixteen to seventeen years old. Do you have any opinions about that . . . do you think that's a normal age? [*daughter shakes head*] You don't know?
DAUGHTER: What do you think?
MOTHER: I think that's young. It's really scary for me to hear.
DAUGHTER: It depends on who it is.
MOTHER: It depends on the kid? Why does it depend?
DAUGHTER: If you're going out with that person . . . or just 'cause you feel like it.
MOTHER: You mean if you have a real relationship with that person or someone you just happen to meet? So you think it makes a difference then?
DAUGHTER: Don't you?
MOTHER: Yeah, I definitely do. I think that some people don't though. [*conversation continues for a couple of minutes*] If somebody asked you to go on a date, would you?
DAUGHTER: Yes!
MOTHER: Has anybody asked you to go on a date by yourself?
DAUGHTER: Mom! You don't go up to someone and say, "Would you go on a date with me by myself!"
MOTHER: Oh.
DAUGHTER: That's so dumb!
MOTHER: What do you do? [*Both laugh.*]
DAUGHTER: No one would ever do that! You don't go on "dates" with people.
MOTHER: You don't go on dates with people. What do you do then?
DAUGHTER: You just go places with them [*laughs*]. You're so annoying!
MOTHER: Well, then you start talking about it. I'll listen.

References

Baumeister, L. M., Flores, E., & Marin, B. V. (1995). Sex information given to Latina adolescents by parents. *Health Education Research, 10,* 233–239.
Burgoon, J. K. (1985). Nonverbal signals. In M. L. Knapp & G. R. Miller (Eds.), *Handbook of interpersonal communication* (pp. 344–390). Thousand Oaks, CA: Sage.
Clawson, C. L., & Reese-Weber, M. (2003). The amount and timing of parent-adolescent sexual communication as predictors of late adolescent sexual risk-taking behaviors. *Journal of Sex Research, 40,* 256–265.
Crawford, M., & Popp, D. (2003). Sexual double standards: A review and methodological critique of two decades of research. *Journal of Sex Research, 40,* 13–26.
D'Augelli, A. R., Hershberger, S. L., & Pilkington, N. W. (1998). Lesbian, gay, and bisexual youth and their families: Disclosure of sexual orientation and its consequences. *American Journal of Orthopsychiatry, 68,* 361–371.
DiIorio, C., Kelley, M., & Hockenberry-Eaton, M. (1999). Communication about sexual issues: Mothers, fathers, and friends. *Journal of Adolescent Health, 24,* 181–189.
East, P. L. (1996). The younger sisters of childbearing adolescents: Their attitudes, expectations, and behaviors. *Child Development, 67,* 267–282.

Feldman, S. S., Turner, R. A., & Araujo, K. (1999). Interpersonal context as an influence on sexual timetables of youths: Gender and ethnic effects. *Journal of Research on Adolescence, 9*, 25–52.

Fisher, T. D. (1986). An exploratory study of parent-child communication about sex and the attitudes of early, middle, and late adolescents. *Journal of Genetic Psychology, 147,* 543–557.

Fox, G. L., & Inazu, J. K. (1980). Patterns and outcomes of mother-daughter communication about sexuality. *Journal of Social Issues, 36,* 7–27.

Guzmán, B. L., Schlehofer-Sutton, M. M., Villanueva, C. M., Stritto, M.E.D., Casad, B. J., & Feria, A. (2003). Let's talk about sex: How comfortable discussions about sex impact teen sexual behavior. *Journal of Health Communication, 8,* 583–598.

Handelsman, C. D., Cabral, R. J., & Weisfeld, G. E. (1987). Sources of information and adolescent sexual knowledge and behavior. *Journal of Adolescent Research, 2,* 455–463.

Hillier, L. (2002). "It's a catch-22": Same-sex attracted young people on coming out to parents. In S. S. Feldman & D. A. Rosenthal (Eds.), *Talking sexuality: Parent-adolescent communication* (pp. 75–92). San Francisco: Jossey-Bass.

Hutchinson, M. K., Jemmott, J. B., Jemmott, L. S., Braverman, P., & Fong, G.T. (2003). The role of mother-daughter sexual risk communication in reducing sexual risk behaviors among urban adolescent females: A prospective study. *Journal of Adolescent Health, 33,* 98–107.

Jaccard, J., Dittus, P. J., & Gordon, V. V. (1996). Maternal correlates of adolescent sexual and contraceptive behavior. *Family Planning Perspectives, 28,* 159–185.

Jaccard, J., Dittus, P. J., & Gordon, V. V. (1998). Parent-adolescent congruency in reports of adolescent sexual behavior and in communications about sexual behavior. *Child Development, 69,* 247–261.

Jacoby, L. (1978). On interpreting the effects of repetition: Solving a problem versus remembering a solution. *Journal of Verbal Learning and Verbal Behavior, 17,* 649–667.

Kotva, H. J., & Schneider, H. G. (1990). Those "talks"—General and sexual communication between mothers and daughters. *Journal of Social Behavior and Personality, 5,* 603–613.

Lefkowitz, E. S., Boone, T. L., Au, T. K., & Sigman, M. (2003). No sex or safe sex? Mothers' and adolescents' discussions about abstinence and safer sex. *Health Education Research, 18,* 341–351.

Lefkowitz, E. S., Boone, T. L., Sigman, M. D., & Au, T. K. (2002). He said, she said: Gender differences in self-reported and observed conversations about sexuality. *Journal of Research on Adolescence, 12,* 217–242.

Lefkowitz, E. S., & Espinosa-Hernandez, G. (2006). *Sex-related communication with mothers and close friends during the transition to university.* Unpublished manuscript.

Lefkowitz, E. S., Kahlbaugh, P., & Sigman, M. (1996). Turn-taking in mother-adolescent conversations about sexuality and conflict. *Journal of Youth and Adolescence, 25,* 307–321.

Lefkowitz, E. S., Romo, L., Corona, R., Au, T. K., & Sigman, M. (2000). How Latino-American and European-American adolescents discuss conflicts, sexuality, and AIDS with their mothers. *Developmental Psychology, 36,* 315–325.

Lefkowitz, E. S., Sigman, M., & Au, T. K. (2000). Helping mothers discuss sexuality and AIDS with adolescents. *Child Development, 71,* 1383–1394.

Moore, K. A., Peterson, J. L., & Furstenberg, F. F. (1986). Parental attitudes and the occurrence of early sexual activity. *Journal of Marriage and the Family, 48,* 777–782.

Orgocka, A. (2004). Perceptions of communication and education about sexuality among Muslim immigrant girls in the U.S. *Sex Education, 3,* 255–271.

Raffaelli, M., Bogenschneider, K., & Flood, M. F. (1998). Parent-teen communication about sexual topics. *Journal of Family Issues, 19,* 315–333.

Raffaelli, M., & Ontai, L. (2001). "She's 16 years old and there's boys calling over to the house": An exploratory study of sexual socialization in Latino families. *Culture, Health, and Sexuality, 3,* 295–310.

Raffaelli, M., Smart, L. A., Van Horn, S. C., Hohbein, A. D., Klein, J. E., & Chan, W. L. (1999). Do mothers and teens disagree about sexual communication? A methodological reappraisal. *Journal of Youth and Adolescence, 28,* 395–402.

Rosenthal, D. A., & Feldman, S. S. (1999). The importance of importance: The differentiated nature of parent-adolescent communication about sexuality. *Journal of Adolescence, 22,* 835–852.

Savin-Williams, R. C., & Dubé, E. M. (1998). Parental reactions to their child's disclosure of a gay/lesbian identity. *Family Relations: Interdisciplinary Journal of Applied Family Studies, 47,* 7–13.

Shearer, C. L., Hosterman, S. J., Gillen, M. M., & Lefkowitz, E. S. (2005). Are traditional gender roles associated with risky sexual behavior and attitudes about condom use? *Sex Roles, 52,* 311–324.

Ward, L. M., Hansbrough, E., & Walker, E. (2005). Contributions of music video exposure to Black adolescents' gender and sexual schemas. *Journal of Adolescent Research, 20,* 143–166.

White, C. P., Wright, D. W., & Barnes, H. L. (1995). Correlates of parent-child communication about specific sexual topics: A study of rural parents with school-aged children. *Personal Relationships, 2,* 327–343.

EVA S. LEFKOWITZ is associate professor of human development and family studies at Pennsylvania State University.

TARA M. STOPPA is a graduate student in the Department of Human Development and Family Studies at the Pennsylvania State University.

NEW DIRECTIONS FOR CHILD AND ADOLESCENT DEVELOPMENT • DOI: 10.1002/cad

5

This chapter discusses several ways in which the media may serve as a positive force in young women's sexual health and development through the information and models they provide and the opportunities they offer for validation and self-expression.

Uncommonly Good: Exploring How Mass Media May Be a Positive Influence on Young Women's Sexual Health and Development

L. Monique Ward, Kyla M. Day, Marina Epstein

By most accounts, popular media are perceived to play a critical role in the sexual socialization of American youth. Children aged eight to eighteen are reported to use the media nearly eight hours each day, devoting three to four hours to TV viewing alone (Roberts, Foehr, & Rideout, 2005). These numbers are even higher for Black and Latino youth and for younger teens than for older teens. At the same time, analyses indicate that popular media are saturated with sexual content and imagery, which appear in 83 percent of programs popular among adolescents (Kunkel et al., 2003), 44 to 76 percent of music videos (Ward, 2003), and 29 percent of the interactions of TV characters (Ward, 1995).

The messages conveyed about sexuality are not always ideal, however, and they are often limited, unrealistic, and stereotypical. Dominating is a recreational orientation to sexuality in which courtship is treated as a competition, a battle of the sexes, characterized by dishonesty, game playing, and manipulation (Ward, 1995). Also prominent are stereotypical sexual roles featuring women as sexual objects, whose value is based solely on their physical appearance, and men as sex-driven players looking to "score" at all costs (Arnett, 2002; Gow, 1995; Grauerholz & King, 1997; Ward, 1995). Given that cultivation theorists argue that the more time we spend

consuming media, the more likely we are to accept its fictional images as reality (Gerbner, Gross, Morgan, & Signorielli, 1994), it is likely that teens who frequently view TV's repeated portrayals of glamorous, casual, risk-free sex and of objectified women and irresponsible men will gradually come to adopt similar beliefs about sex in the real world.

Evidence accumulated from multiple fields indicates that such speculations may be valid. Across several studies, frequent viewing of sexually oriented genres, such as soap operas and music videos, has been associated with a greater acceptance of common sexual stereotypes (for example, that women are sexual objects) and with dysfunctional beliefs about relationships (Haferkamp, 1999; Walsh-Childers & Brown, 1993; Ward, 2002). Experimental results support these findings, showing that women exposed to sexual and sexist media content offer stronger endorsement than do women exposed to nonsexual content of casual and stereotypical attitudes about sex (Johnson, Adams, Ashburn, & Reed, 1995; Ward, 2002; Ward, Hansbrough, & Walker, 2005). Links have also been found to viewers' beliefs about sexual norms. More specifically, frequent exposure to sexually oriented genres leads younger viewers to overestimate the prevalence of divorce, extramarital affairs, and sexually active youth, creating the notion that "everyone is doing it" (Buerkel-Rothfuss & Strouse, 1993; Davis & Mares, 1998; Ward, 2002). Such findings demonstrate the likely problematic influences of media exposure on emergent beliefs about sexuality.

But we also know that the picture is not this clear-cut. There are several indications that such negative outcomes are neither guaranteed nor universal. First, findings indicate that media content is not uniformly negative. Information about sexual health, risks, and thoughtful decision making is sometimes present. Indeed, 60 percent of teens surveyed said that they learned how to say no to a sexual situation by watching television, and 43 percent said they learned something about how to talk to a partner about safer sex (Collins, Elliott, Berry, Kanouse, & Hunter, 2003). Second, despite evidence that a majority of portrayals are one-dimensional sexual stereotypes, some characters are not and instead provide realistic characterizations with which viewers can connect. For example, undergraduates still speak of the relevance of fifteen-year-old Angela Chase (from My So-Called Life), some ten years after the series was initially cancelled. Third, evidence suggests that media content may offer youth opportunities to set relationship ideals and practice relationship dynamics vicariously, through celebrity crushes and teen idols. Indeed, some consider media use and selection to be a key component of adolescent identity work (Arnett, 1995). Finally, new media genres such as zines offer young women the opportunity to express themselves sexually by reporting on their own perspectives and resisting societal constraints.

Our goal is to broaden perspectives on media effects to consider their potential positive contributions to female sexual health and development. Drawing from criteria developed by the Sexuality Information and Education Council of the United States (SIECUS), we conceptualize positive sexual health and development as sexuality that is consensual, honest, mutually pleasurable, nonexploitative, and protected against unintended pregnancy and sexually transmitted diseases (STDs). We also view sexuality and sexual pleasure as natural parts of women's lives and seek as ideals greater sexual agency, body comfort, openness to sexual-minority women, accurate exchanges of sexual information, and acceptance of both coital and noncoital practices. We discuss here ways in which the media may help meet these ideals and define the mass media to include television programming, movies, magazines, the Internet, video games, and music. We first present four positive media contributions and then close with suggestions for additional modifications.

Positive Contribution 1: Media Can Offer Sexual Information

Learning about sexuality is a complex, multidimensional process that involves incorporating diverse information from multiple sources. The input received takes many forms, including facts, values, norms, opinions, and personal experiences. Compelling examples of each form can be found in media outlets.

Sexual Health Content in Popular, Mainstream Magazines. One way in which media content may serve as a positive influence on sexual health and development is in the sharing of information about sexual health issues. Magazines in particular are often sought out for this reason. Adolescent and young adult readers indicate that they turn to magazines as a valued source of advice about their personal lives (Kaiser Family Foundation, 2004) and for information about reproductive health when confidentiality is an issue (Treise & Gotthoffer, 2002). Indeed, 51 percent of readers aged twelve to eighteen surveyed in one study identified magazines as an important source of information on reproductive and sexual health (Kaiser Family Foundation, 1996). Magazines are likely to be an ideal source in this domain for several reasons. First, they can be consumed relatively privately and anonymously. Young women can examine these media in the privacy of their own rooms without having to ask personal questions directly and risk embarrassment. Also, because reading magazines is a normative action, purchasing them is guilt and taboo free. Second, magazines are portable and highly accessible, available for multiple reviews and continued referencing. Third, magazines address their readers directly and intimately, often using *you*. By striking a more intimate and familiar tone, magazines connect with adolescent women who may be feeling particularly self-conscious or disconnected at this developmental stage. In these ways, magazines provide opportunities for young women to learn about serious issues without serious consequences.

Although not the dominant sexual content carried, analyses indicate that magazine coverage of sexual health issues does occur and has increased in some respects over the past decades. In her 1997 analysis of four leading teen magazines (*Seventeen, YM, Sassy,* and *Teen*), Signorielli reported that

3 percent of all articles focused on STDs, 2 percent on pregnancy, and 2 percent on contraception. In their study of thirty-two magazines popular with twelve to fourteen year olds, Pardun, L'Engle, and Brown (2005) found that 8 percent of all magazine units (paragraphs and headlines) included sexual content and that 4 percent of such content contained information about sexual health, defined as references to physical/sexual development, refusal of advances/abstinence, masturbation, STDs, negative emotional consequences, condoms, and contraception. Whereas it is true that such content focuses more on the risks of sex than on its pleasures, thereby supporting traditional gender discourses (Fine, 1988; Tolman, 1999), magazines do offer young women information (for example, how to identify an STD) they may be reluctant to seek elsewhere.

Others have compared magazines' coverage of sexual health content to their coverage of information about sexual behavior and activities. In an analysis of the features and columns in women's, men's, and teen magazines from 1995 to 1996, Walsh-Childers, Treise, and Gotthoffer (1997) found that 34 percent of all articles on a sexual issue focused on sexual health; this was the case for 28 percent of the articles in men's magazines and 42 percent in teen magazines. Sexual health topics were defined here as those related to contraception, pregnancy (both planned and unintended), abortion, emergency contraception, STDs, and HIV/AIDS. In their study of four popular teen magazines and twelve popular women's magazines published between 1986 and 1996, Walsh-Childers, Gotthoffer, and Lepre (2002) found that overall, 48.4 percent of the sex-related items in teen magazines and 47.2 percent in women's magazines focused on sexual health and reproductive care issues. Dominant among the issues discussed were pregnancy and contraception. Similar analyses of five African American and sixteen Latino magazines indicated that 30 percent of the sex- or health-related articles in African American magazines covered sexual and reproductive health topics, as did 45 percent of the 324 articles coded from the Latino magazines (Johnson, Gotthoffer, & Lauffer, 1999). Thus, although further study is needed concerning the impact of this content on women's health knowledge and behavior, evidence does indicate that young women can get information about a range of sexual health topics from magazines.

Entertainment-Education. A second pathway through which media content may pass on information about sexual health issues is through entertainment-education. As defined by Singhal and Rogers (1999), entertainment-education is "the process of purposely designing and implementing a media message both to entertain and educate, in order to increase audience members' knowledge about an educational issue, create favorable attitudes, and change overt behavior" (p. 9). The goal is to capitalize on the appeal of popular media, such as soap operas and radio dramas, in order to show individuals how they can live safer, healthier, and happier lives. Through exposure to positive, negative, and transitional characters (those in the process of changing their errant ways), audience members can acquire information about health issues and model characters who are similar to themselves. This strategy has been enacted successfully in television since 1951 in several countries worldwide. Common goals have been the promotion of family planning, equality for women, literacy, and HIV prevention.

Evidence from entertainment-education programs conducted around the globe indicates that carefully designed entertainment media can help educate audiences about sexual health issues, promote prosocial behavior, and be economically profitable. For example, a radio drama entitled *Twende na Wakati* (*Let's Go with the Times*), which aired from 1993 to 1998 in Tanzania, was found to have strong effects on family planning and HIV prevention attitudes and behavior (Singhal & Rogers, 1999). Compared with those who did not receive this radio broadcast, residents in the treatment areas increased their sense of self-efficacy with respect to family size determination, increased approval for contraceptive use, increased interspousal communication about family planning, and increased current practice of family planning. Later programming that focused on HIV prevention was found to reduce the number of sexual partners of both women and men and to increase condom adoption (Vaughan, Rogers, Singhal, & Swalehe, 2000). Similar increases in knowledge, positive attitudes, and use of family planning methods have been reported in at least twelve studies (as summarized by Singhal & Rogers, 1999), as a consequence of exposure to programming such as the radio drama series *Fakube Jarra* (Wise Man) in the Gambia (Valente, Kim, Lettenmaier, Glass, & Dibba, 1994), the radio soap *Apwe Plezi* (connotes the notion "After the pleasure comes the pain") in St. Lucia (Vaughan, Regis, & St. Catherine, 2000), and the TV drama *In a Lighter Mood* in Nigeria (Piotrow et al., 1990).

Could something like this work in the United States? Skepticism is typically the first response to this question due to the expansiveness of American media outlets, their commercial rather than government ownership, and the abundance of competing messages and sources of entertainment. However, efforts addressing a number of sexual health issues have in fact been implemented in this country (outside PBS). Most notable are collaborative efforts among the Kaiser Family Foundation, the Centers for Disease Control, and television writers that have proven successful in promoting sexual health. For example, mention of the sexually transmitted disease human papillomavirus or HPV and its link to cervical cancer in one *ER* episode produced a significantly greater awareness of this condition among viewers surveyed both the following day and six weeks later (Kaiser Family Foundation, 2000). In August 2001, the National STD and AIDS Hotline numbers were displayed at the end of two episodes of a popular soap opera (*The Bold and the Beautiful*) that had just included an HIV-prevention storyline. Findings indicate that call volumes rose dramatically in the hour following the broadcast, increasing from 88 calls the day before to 1,426 the day of the broadcast (Kennedy, O'Leary, Beck, Pollard, & Simpson, 2004). When information about emergency contraception was included in one episode of *ER*, telephone surveys revealed a substantial increase in the number of regular *ER* viewers who could accurately define this method and explain how to access it (Kaiser Family Foundation, 2000). Similarly, when information about condom effectiveness rates was incorporated into an episode of *Friends*, confirmed teen viewers were more likely than nonviewers to later provide accurate information about this statistic (Collins et al., 2003). Thus, whereas entertainment-education programming and research are not without their limitations (for a review, see Sherry, 1997), with appropriate efforts by appropriate parties, important sexual health information can be inserted in U.S. media, with beneficial consequences.

Positive Contribution 2: Media Can Offer Diverse Sexual Models

Although most assessments of the impact of media use have focused on the role of exposure levels, based on premises of the cultivation model, exposure is only one dimension of media use and therefore only one pathway of potential influence. Indeed, media use is not a passive experience. Media users select particular content from a growing array of options and construct media diets that speak to their individual needs, identities, and experiences (Steele, 1999). Accordingly, some theoretical approaches, including Greenberg's drench hypothesis (Greenberg, 1988), underscore the role of viewer identification, arguing that media portrayals with which viewers connect and identify will exert the most influence. Here, it is argued that specific critical portrayals may exert a stronger force on impression formation and image building than might the sheer frequency of television viewed. This notion emphasizes the power of individual performances to affect viewers, acknowledging that media portrayals differ in their depth, strength, and authenticity. In this way, rare but positive portrayals of female sexuality could have a deep effect on the viewer and could overwhelm, or "drench," the contributions of more everyday or stereotyped roles (Graves, 1999). It is therefore critical that we examine not only students' media exposure levels, but also the extent to which they identify and connect with specific characters.

Criticisms of viewer selection and identification mechanisms typically center on the limited nature of media content, offering skepticism, for example, that portrayals are actually diverse enough to provide anything but mainstream options and messages to young viewers. Are portrayals of female sexuality diverse enough to provide varied role models? Focus group and interview data suggest that viewers seem to manage quite well, selecting particular models that match their personalities and interests and viewing the same models differently based on their own preexisting perspectives. For example, in one interview study exploring forces shaping adult women's sexual development (Ward & Wyatt, 1994), many participants cited the influence of Lucy from *I Love Lucy*. Some women saw her as smart, resourceful, and determined and aspired to be like her. Others saw Lucy as ditzy and subservient and made efforts *not* to be like her. Either way, Lucy served as an anchor point for women's reflections on their own sexual development.

Similar diverse models and perspectives appear in our current research. Over the past several years, we have included the following question on our surveys to undergraduates: "What character on TV do you most identify with?" The responses accumulated thus far from 1,761 students speak to the diversity of portrayals available (Ward, Smiler, Caruthers, & Merriwether, 2006). Table 5.1 presents the top twelve favorites offered by the women surveyed. From this table, we see that young women select a range of characters who speak to them, from the young and virginal, such as Angela Chase on *My So-Called Life* or Lisa Simpson from *The Simpsons*, to the more sexually free and outspoken, such as Ally McBeal or Carrie on *Sex and the City*— and these are only the characters who received at least ten mentions. In addition to these top twelve nominees, 149 other characters, ranging from Claire Huxtable of *The Cosby Show* to Buffy, the Vampire Slayer, each received between one and ten mentions. These data demonstrate some diversity in the representations of femininity and female sexuality provided by mainstream media. Young women do select and connect with particular portrayals, who likely serve as role models and guideposts of relationship dynamics.

Is there any evidence that viewers use media characters as models of sexual behavior? Findings from survey data indicate that identifying with popular characters and perceiving media figures as role models is indeed associated with students' sexual attitudes and behavior. For example, Fabes and Strouse (1987) found that undergraduates choosing a media figure or peer as a model of sexual behavior reported more frequent intercourse than those selecting parent or educator models. Similarly, Ward and Friedman (2006) report that stronger identification with popular TV characters is

Table 5.1. Top Twelve Favorite TV Characters of Undergraduate Women Surveyed

Female Character	Number of Nominations
1. Felicity on *Felicity*	107
2. Joey on *Dawson's Creek*	95
3. Rachel on *Friends*	63
4. Angela on *My So-Called Life*	52
5. Ally on *Ally McBeal*	48
6. Monica on *Friends*	46
7. Phoebe on *Friends*	21
8. Daria on *Daria*	19
9. Lisa Simpson on *The Simpsons*	18
10. Kelly Taylor on *Beverly Hills 90210*	16
11. Grace on *Will and Grace*	14
12. Carrie on *Sex and the City*	11

associated with higher levels of sexual experience among high school students. Findings indicate that connections also exist to students' sexual attitudes and expectations. Among undergraduate women, for example, stronger identification with popular media portrayals is associated with higher expectations of the level of sexual activity of one's peers (Ward & Rivadeneyra, 1999). And among high school girls, stronger identification with more objectifying music artists is associated with greater support of sexually objectifying attitudes toward women, and stronger identification with less objectifying music artists is associated with less support of these attitudes (Gordon, 2004). Evidence therefore indicates that young women's sexual attitudes and behavior do parallel the particular characters with whom they most connect. Whether they identify with a particular character and seek to behave accordingly or are drawn to media figures who match their existing ideals and behaviors, having a diverse selection of models provides space for young women to draw validation of their differing sensibilities, fears, and aspirations.

Positive Contribution 3: Media Offer Vicarious Practice of Dating Norms and Ideals

In considering possible positive influences of media use, it is important to consider not only that certain content may be more beneficial than other content, but also that certain audiences may be more open to influence than others. Media constructionists and media use models (Steele, 1999) acknowledge that a viewer's starting point and particular needs play an important role in shaping how she perceives and makes use of media content. In terms of sexual content, it is therefore likely that adolescent women at different stages of pubertal and sexual development bring different needs to the media and may draw different interpretations of the content.

In early adolescence and in the early stages of pubertal development, girls are beginning to explore what it means to be female and what it means to be sexual. One benefit of media content at this time is that it provides a means for young women to try out romantic scripts in their imagination, allowing them to conceptualize themselves enacting the script (Arnett, 1995). For example, fantasizing about media characters (idols) allows girls to experience a fantasy relationship with idols on television without concerns that they will be rejected or will have to engage in activities for which they are not ready (Karniol, 2001). Evidence suggests that these fantasy crushes may serve as a placeholder for actual same-age boys (or girls), in that girls who are interested in media idols prefer idols who are in a somewhat attainable age range (Brown, White, & Nikopoulou, 1993). These girls are not delusional, however, and are aware of differences between media and reality and between the idol and real-life crushes. For these girls, the idols are not perceived as real, and the girls are not using the media as an exact guide, but perhaps as a way in which to fantasize about, conceptualize, and

NEW DIRECTIONS FOR CHILD AND ADOLESCENT DEVELOPMENT • DOI: 10.1002/cad

practice behavior that would not yet be possible in their real lives. Thus, media idols allow girls to fantasize about a person without real-life concerns or consequences, such as rejection or coercion.

On the other end of the spectrum, sexual content in the media may serve a useful function for early-maturing girls whose peers have not yet reached this point in their pubertal development. Emerging findings indicate that such girls are drawn to sexual media content. For example, in their ethnographic study of twenty girls aged eleven to fifteen, Brown et al. (1993) found that girls who were more biologically developed than their peers were more likely to seek out sexual images and information in the media. Testing this issue with survey data, Brown, Halpern, and L'Engle (2005) discovered that regardless of age or race, earlier-maturing girls expressed more interest than later-maturing girls in seeing sexual content in TV, movies, and magazines and in listening to sexual content in music. These girls were also more likely to be consuming media with sexual content. The authors speculate that for these girls, the media may serve as a kind of "super-peer" because early-maturing girls are not able to turn to their actual peers for information or norm setting. They may be looking for information in the media because their real-life peers are not yet as interested in sexual issues as they are. In these ways, media figures may allow young girls to practice crushes and allow early-maturing girls possible sexual examples, norms, and information as they wait for their peers to catch up.

We acknowledge that these practices may not always be ideal, especially, for example, if idolization sets up unrealistic expectations that cause later disappointment. In addition, using media models for romantic role playing or as super-peers may also reinforce traditional gender scripts that place heterosexual success at the center of the feminine ideal and overemphasize its importance in women's lives. Together, these issues highlight the diverse and important implications of media use by female adolescents.

Positive Contribution 4: Resisting Through Self-Expression

A fourth pathway through which media use may contribute to positive sexual development among women is through the creation and consumption of girl-zines. Girl-zines (or grrrl zines) are self-published, small-circulation publications created by girls and young women to connect with each other, share personal experiences, and raise their voices in resistance to mainstream media. Zines were originally a product of the underground punk movement in the 1970s, with grrrl zines tracing their roots to a movement called Riot Grrrls started in 1991 by young women who felt underrepresented in the punk scene (Duncombe, 1997; Ferris, 2001). Today girl-zines retain their underground nature—they are published in small numbers and are traded or left anonymously in coffee shops and bookstores—and are at once public and private publications. Zines offer a safe format to engage in "a sort of c/overt resistance that allows girls to overtly express their anger, confusion, and frustration publicly to like-minded peers, but still remain covert and anonymous to authority figures" (Schilt, 2003, p. 81).

Authors of girl-zines address many of the same topics that are seen in academic research on girls, including sexuality, feminism, gender, relationships, and puberty (Ferris, 2001; Schilt, 2003). However, zines address these topics in a "confrontational, honest, and frank manner" (Ferris, 2001, p. 52) and offer alternative perspectives of girls' lives, femininity, and female sexuality that move beyond the beauty-centered, heteronormative content of mainstream magazines.

In an in-depth study of more than thirty zines and their writers, Wray and Steele (2002) argue that this personal nature of zines and the more realistic representation of the lives of teenage girls is the zines' greatest achievement. Although zines are primarily produced by White, middle-class teens, they do provide more diversity in representing what it means to be a woman than do traditional media. One young woman referred to the zine culture as "a place to vent, to be accepted, not a place to be ashamed and boy-obsessed" (p. 207).

This girl-driven approach is what makes the zine network especially beneficial for girls and provides an alternative to the "girl-based and consumer-market-driven strategies of girl empowerment" (Schilt, 2003, p. 73). In her study of zines as a form of resistance, Schilt argues that the do-it-yourself framework of zines encourages girls to create their own medium if the one provided to them by the market does not meet their needs. In addition, participating in the zine culture, which is not driven by profit, encourages girls to be more critical consumers of cultural products and provides empowerment for their own ideas. Finally, girl-zines both encourage participation in other political, feminist, and antiracist action and provide information for how to become involved.

Is That Enough? Untapped Potential and a Wish List for Further Positive Portrayals

We see many ways in which media content may be a positive force in young women's sexual health and development by providing information on sexual health issues; offering a diverse array of portrayals to serve as validation, models, and guides; or allowing outlets for resistance and self-expression. At this point, our arguments are mostly speculative, since little empirical evidence demonstrates that these practices are in fact beneficial in the ways presumed. In additional, our analysis focuses on content at the margins and does not directly confront concerns raised about the many existing limited, stereotypical, and objectifying portrayals of female sexuality. We conclude with a wish list of ten changes that mainstream media could make in order to be more beneficial for girls' sexual health and development.

We would like for mainstream media content to include

1. *More three-dimensional characters.* Typically female characters are one-dimensional stereotypes or caricatures (the virgin, the ditz, the slut). We would like to see complex characters who defy labels.
2. *A broader range of physical appearance types and less focus on this as the center of women's worth.* We would like to see women who are comfortable with their bodies. Women's bodies are powerful and can do many things (for example, build, fight, climb, nurture, procreate) and are not just something to look at.
3. *A diminished heteronormative perspective.* We would like to see more three-dimensional portrayals of lesbians, bisexuals, and women questioning their sexuality.
4. *An acknowledgment of gender roles and their constraints on sexuality.* Many portrayals, especially in music videos, treat the sexual double standard as natural and accepted. But traditional gender roles are often quite restrictive. We would like to see portrayals of women and men grappling with these constraints, and perhaps defying them.
5. *More portrayals of "outercourse."* Many movie portrayals go from kissing to intercourse with little in between. There needs to be an acknowledgment of diverse forms of sexual pleasure, including masturbation and manual stimulation.
6. *More agentic portrayals of female sexuality.* Frequently female characters are depicted as waiting for a partner and as accepting whomever comes their way. We would like to see women who have and express their desires, look for respect, and reject partners who are disrespectful.
7. *Portrayals of parents and older adults working to instill sexual agency and sexual self-acceptance within their daughters.*
8. *Women communicating with their partners about sex.* Media portrayals commonly depict women discussing their sexual feelings and exploits with their female friends. We would like these portrayals to expand to include women discussing these issues with their sexual partners.
9. *Portrayals of the ambiguities and negotiations that are involved in navigating sexual relationships.* Sexuality is a journey. Each woman needs to negotiate and discover what works for her, and this answer may vary from partner to partner. We would like to see women (and men) grappling with these ambiguities.
10. *A focus on sexuality not just as a risk for women but also as a site of pleasure.* Young women are typically not taught to develop sexual feelings and to discover their body and its pleasures. It would be beneficial on many levels to show women learning and taking these steps.

We acknowledge that media content is only one of many sources contributing to young women's sexual health and development. We also know that its effects are not wholly under personal control. However, we hope that the analyses and suggestions provided here will provoke both researchers and media makers to think more broadly about the choices that they make and to continue to fight for content that will broaden women's perspectives instead of constrain them.

References

Arnett, J. J. (1995). Adolescents' uses of media for self-socialization. *Journal of Youth and Adolescence, 24,* 519–533.

Arnett, J. J. (2002). The sounds of sex: Sex in teens' music and music videos. In J. Brown, K. Walsh-Childers, & J. Steele (Eds.), *Sexual teens, sexual media* (pp. 253–264). Mahwah, NJ: Erlbaum.

Brown, J. D., Halpern, C. T., & L'Engle, K. (2005). Mass media as a sexual super peer for early maturing girls. *Journal of Adolescent Health, 36,* 420–427.

Brown, J. D., White, A. B., & Nikopoulou, L. (1993). Disinterest, intrigue, resistance: Early adolescent girls' use of sexual media content. In B. S. Greenberg, J. D. Brown, & N. L. Buerkel-Rothfuss (Eds.), *Media, sex, and the adolescent* (pp. 263–276). Cresskill, NJ: Hampton Press.

Buerkel-Rothfuss, N. L., & Strouse, J. S. (1993). Media exposure and perceptions of sexual behaviors: The cultivation hypothesis moves to the bedroom. In B. S. Greenberg, J. D. Brown, & N. L. Buerkel-Rothfuss (Eds.), *Media, sex, and the adolescent* (pp. 225–247). Creskill, NJ: Hampton Press.

Collins, R., Elliott, M., Berry, S., Kanouse, D., & Hunter, S. (2003). Entertainment television as a healthy sex educator: The impact of condom-efficacy information in an episode of *Friends. Pediatrics, 112,* 1115–1121.

Davis, S., & Mares, M.-L. (1998). Effects of talk show viewing on adolescents. *Journal of Communication, 48,* 69–86.

Duncombe, S. (1997). *Notes from underground: Zines and the politics of alternative culture.* London: Verso.

Fabes, R. A., & Strouse, J. (1987). Perceptions of responsible and irresponsible models of sexuality: A correlational study. *Journal of Sex Research, 23,* 70–84.

Ferris, M. A. (2001). Resisting mainstream media: Girls and the act of making zines (young women, feminists, activists, grrls). *Canadian Woman Studies, 20,* 51–56.

Fine, M. (1988). Sexuality, schooling, and adolescent females: The missing discourse of desire. *Harvard Educational Review, 58*(1), 29–53.

Gerbner, G., Gross, L., Morgan, M., & Signorielli, N. (1994). Growing up with television: The cultivation perspective. In J. Bryant & D. Zillman (Eds.), *Media effects: Advances in theory and research* (pp. 17–41). Mahwah, NJ: Erlbaum.

Gordon, M. (2004). *Media images of women and African American girls' sense of self.* Unpublished doctoral dissertation, University of Michigan.

Gow, J. (1995). Reconsidering gender roles on MTV: Depictions in the most popular music videos on the early 1990s. *Communication Reports, 9,* 151–161.

Grauerholz, E., & King, A. (1997). Primetime sexual harassment. *Violence Against Women, 3,* 129–148.

Graves, S. B. (1999). Television and prejudice reduction: When does television as a vicarious experience make a difference? *Journal of Social Issues, 55,* 707–727.

Greenberg, B. S. (1988). Some uncommon television images and the drench hypothesis. In S. Oskamp (Ed.), *Television as a social issue* (pp. 88–102). Thousand Oaks, CA: Sage.

Haferkamp, C. J. (1999). Beliefs about relationships in relation to television viewing, soap opera viewing, and self-monitoring. *Current Psychology, 18,* 193–204.

Johnson, J., Adams, M. S., Ashburn, L., & Reed, W. (1995). Differential gender effects of exposure to rap music on African American adolescents' acceptance of teen dating violence. *Sex Roles, 33*, 597–605.

Johnson, M. A., Gotthoffer, A. R., & Lauffer, K. (1999). The sexual and reproductive content of African American and Latino magazines. *Howard Journal of Communication, 10*, 169–187.

Kaiser Family Foundation (1996). *Teens on sex: What they say about the media as an information source.* Menlo Park, CA: Author.

Kaiser Family Foundation. (2000). *Teens and sex: The role of popular television, fact sheet.* Menlo Park, CA: Author.

Kaiser Family Foundation. (2004). *Tweens, teens, and magazines: Fact Sheet.* Menlo Park, CA: Author.

Karniol, R. (2001). Adolescent females' idolization of male media stars as a transition into sexuality. *Sex Roles, 44*, 61–77.

Kennedy, M. G., O'Leary, A., Beck, V., Pollard, K., & Simpson, P. (2004). Increases in calls to the CDC National STD and AIDS Hotline following AIDS-related episodes in a soap opera. *Journal of Communication, 54*, 287–301.

Kunkel, D., Eyal, K., Biely, E., Cope-Farrar, K., Donnerstein, E., & Fandrich, R. (2003). *Sex on TV 3: A biennial report to the Kaiser Family Foundation.* Menlo Park, CA: Kaiser Family Foundation.

Pardun, C. J., L'Engle, K. L., & Brown, J. D. (2005). Linking exposure to outcomes: Early adolescents' consumption of sexual content in six media. *Mass Communication and Society, 8*, 75-91.

Piotrow, P., Rimon, J. G., Winnard, K., Kincaid, L., Huntington, D., & Convisser, J. (1990). Mass media family planning promotion in three Nigerian cities. *Studies in Family Planning, 21*, 265–274.

Roberts, D., Foehr, U., & Rideout, V. (2005, March). *Generation M: Media in the lives of 8–18 year olds.* Menlo Park, CA: Henry J. Kaiser Family Foundation.

Schilt, K. (2003). "I'll resist with every inch and every breath": Girls and zine making as a form of resistance. *Youth and Society, 35*, 71–97.

Sherry, J. L. (1997). Prosocial soap operas for development: A review of research and theory. *Journal of International Communication, 4*, 75–100.

Signorielli, N. (1997). *Reflections of girls in the media: A content analysis across six media.* Oakland and Menlo Park, CA: Children NOW and Kaiser Family Foundation.

Singhal, A., & Rogers, E. M. (1999). *Entertainment-education: A communication strategy for social change.* Mahwah, NJ: Erlbaum.

Steele, J. R. (1999). Teenage sexuality and media practice: Factoring in the influences of family, friends, and school. *Journal of Sex Research, 36*, 331–341.

Tolman, D. L. (1999). Female adolescent sexuality in relational context: Beyond sexual decision making. In N. G. Johnson, M. C. Roberts, & J. Worell (Eds.), *Beyond appearance: A new look at adolescent girls* (pp. 227–246). Washington, DC: American Psychological Association.

Treise, D., & Gotthoffer, A. (2002). Stuff you couldn't ask your parents: Teens talking about using magazines for sex information. In J. Brown, K. Walsh-Childers, & J. Steele (Eds.), *Sexual teens, sexual media* (pp. 173–189). Mahwah, NJ: Erlbaum.

Valente, T., Kim, Y., Lettenmaier, C., Glass, W., & Dibba, Y. (1994). Radio promotion of family planning in the Gambia. *International Family Planning Perspectives, 20*, 96–100.

Vaughn, P., Regis, A., & St. Catherine, E. (2000). Effects of an entertainment-education radio soap opera on family planning and HIV prevention in St. Lucia. *International Family Planning Perspectives, 26*, 148–157.

Vaughn, P., Rogers, E., Singhal, A., & Swalehe, R. (2000). Entertainment-education and HIV/AIDS prevention: A field experiment in Tanzania. *Journal of Health Communication, 5*, 81–100.

Walsh-Childers, K., & Brown, J. D. (1993). Adolescents' acceptance of sex-role stereotypes and television viewing. In B. S. Greenberg, J. D. Brown, & N. L. Buerkel-Rothfuss (Eds.), *Media, sex, and the adolescent* (pp. 117–133). Creskill, NJ: Hampton Press.

Walsh-Childers, K., Gotthoffer, A., & Lepre, C. R. (2002). From "Just the Facts" to "Downright Salacious": Teens' and women's magazine coverage of sex and sexual health. In J. D. Brown, J. R. Steele, & K. Walsh-Childers (Eds.), *Sexual teens, sexual media* (pp. 153–172). Mahwah, NJ: Erlbaum.

Walsh-Childers, K., Treise, D., & Gotthoffer, A. (1997). *Sexual health coverage in women's, men's, teen, and other specialty magazines: A current-year and ten-year retrospective content analysis.* Menlo Park, CA: Henry J. Kaiser Family Foundation.

Ward, L. M. (1995). Talking about sex: Common themes about sexuality in the prime-time television programs children and adolescents view most. *Journal of Youth and Adolescence, 24,* 595–615.

Ward, L. M. (2002). Does television exposure affect emerging adults' attitudes and assumptions about sexual relationships? Correlational and experimental confirmation. *Journal of Youth and Adolescence, 31,* 1–15.

Ward, L. M. (2003). Understanding the role of entertainment in the sexual socialization of American youth: A review of empirical research. *Developmental Review, 23,* 347–388.

Ward, L. M., & Friedman, K. (2006). Using TV as a guide: Associations between television viewing and adolescents' sexual attitudes and behavior. *Journal of Research on Adolescence, 16,* 133-156.

Ward, L. M., Hansbrough, E., & Walker, E. (2005). Contributions of music video exposure to Black adolescents' gender and sexual schemas. *Journal of Adolescent Research, 20,* 143–166.

Ward, L. M., & Rivadeneyra, R. (1999). Contributions of entertainment television to adolescents' sexual attitudes and expectations: The role of viewing amount versus viewer involvement. *Journal of Sex Research, 36,* 237–249.

Ward, L. M., Smiler, A., Caruthers, A., & Merriwether, A. (2006). *Mining for mechanisms linking television use and viewers' sexual belief systems.* Unpublished manuscript.

Ward, L. M., & Wyatt, G. (1994). The effects of childhood sexual messages on African-American and White women's adolescent sexual behavior. *Psychology of Women Quarterly, 18,* 183–201.

Wray, J., & Steele, J. (2002). Girls in print: Figuring out what it means to be a girl. In J. D. Brown, J. R. Steele, & K. Walsh-Childers (Eds.), *Sexual teens, sexual media* (pp. 191–208). Mahwah, NJ: Erlbaum.

L. MONIQUE WARD is associate professor of psychology at the University of Michigan.

KYLA M. DAY is a doctoral student in the developmental psychology program at the University of Michigan.

MARINA EPSTEIN is a doctoral student in the combined program of psychology and education at the University of Michigan.

NEW DIRECTIONS FOR CHILD AND ADOLESCENT DEVELOPMENT • DOI: 10.1002/cad

6

This chapter challenges forthcoming research on adolescent female sexuality to take more seriously the role of dominant cultural ideologies regarding heterosexuality and to consider its theoretical and methodological implications.

In a Different Position: Conceptualizing Female Adolescent Sexuality Development Within Compulsory Heterosexuality

Deborah L. Tolman

Skepticism from a Heretic

At my first interview for an academic job, I presented findings from my qualitative phenomenological study of adolescent girls' experiences of sexual desire. To illustrate my finding of the "dilemma of desire" and how some girls sacrifice their desire to keep themselves safe, I described one seventeen-year-old girl (Latina, poor) who loved to dance yet solved the dilemma of her desire by "telling her body 'no.'" She described no longer dancing with boys, because the possibility of her "getting, I'd say, horny" would preclude her ability to keep his sexual excitement in check. Thus, she concluded her desire would inevitably lead down the unavoidably slippery slope to unprotected sexual intercourse, a bad reputation and "disrespect," unwanted pregnancy, and HIV/AIDS.

Special thanks to Celeste Hirschman, Jessica Fields, Lynn Sorsoli, Kathy Goodman, Luis Ubinas, and my 2005 graduate seminar in human sexuality studies at San Francisco State University for thoughtful comments and helpful conversations.

My interpretation was that this girl's formulation of her situation and thus her resolution of it were problematic. She assumed that intercourse was the only sexual outcome. She was responsible for controlling boys' unstoppable desire. Being a desiring girl guaranteed her the moniker and mistreatment of "ho." Should she decide to have sex, the possibility of protection did not seem available to her. I argued that a girl should not have to sacrifice the pleasures of dancing or desire to keep safe. Living her story could diminish her self-knowledge and self-esteem, her ability to have authentic relationships, and to make safe and (what was I thinking?) pleasurable decisions. There I was, innovatively busting out of the straitjacket of risky behavior as the only legitimate question about female sexuality.

My presentation was met with incredulity spiced with derision: "Didn't that girl make the right choice?" asked one search committee member. "She did the responsible thing by avoiding boys' demands for sex. Can you show us some empirical data?" Any feminist with a heartbeat would know that phenomenological data are empirical—meaning knowledge gained through experience, especially the senses. I had met my audience, and it was not me. This perspective on female adolescent sexuality development—that desire, embodied feelings, and sexual subjectivity should be developmentally expected—was radical in the early 1990s; positive female adolescent sexuality was anathema, "culturally unintelligible" (Butler, 1990, p. 42); qualitative methods were heretical, not psychology.

I carry my battle scars proudly. I am witness to and a participant in what may be a sea change in how adolescent researchers conceptualize female adolescent sexuality. Sexual agency, sexual desire, and entitlement to sexuality are increasingly being identified as developmentally salient for girls. Moving into the mainstream is a sign of accomplishment. Feminist theorists and researchers have long been demanding and demonstrating the importance of sexuality—in its plethora of permutations—in girls' development and women's lives. And yet I feel a crisis looming.

The Chinese symbol for crisis reflects its inherent contradiction: risk and opportunity. The presumption of this volume—that positive adolescent female sexuality development is a credible topic—seems at once a brilliant subterfuge—and also a risky move. My delight with a burgeoning mainstream literature on positive adolescent sexuality is peppered with skepticism. This discomfort is part disbelief and part awareness of "the regulatory elements of [the] public emergence of a discourse of [girls'] desire . . . [that has been] appropriated and misused" (Harris, 2005, p. 39). The swift swinging of the pendulum from negative to positive makes me giddy but dubious. To displace the goal of mapping and preventing risk—an absence of "bad"—with positing positive paths—a presence of "good"—may ultimately collude in the whitewashing of multiplying forms of complexity in female adolescents' developing sexuality.

NEW DIRECTIONS FOR CHILD AND ADOLESCENT DEVELOPMENT • DOI: 10.1002/cad

We've Arrived! And It's Really Frightening . . .

The caveat is the neutering of sexuality that seems to accompany a move into the mainstream; gender (even as it is exploded by rebellious gender "performances") is already being obscured. In a two-volume issue of the journal *Sexuality Research and Public Policy* dedicated to "Positive Adolescent Sexuality," the (very compelling) introduction is about "adolescent sexuality"; neither the word nor the idea of gender ever appears (Russell, 2005). Going mainstream still incurs the cost of universalizing. Inquiring about gender differences may be a legitimate, even encouraged, enterprise, but entering the mainstream with a gendered conception of sexuality is not. While I am not suggesting that gender is the sole dimension of significance in the development of female adolescent sexuality by any means (Rubin, 1984), I am insisting that it is foundational. It is not happenstance that this volume is dedicated to *female* adolescent sexuality and its development. The persistence of patriarchy demands it.

In my own work and that of other feminists whose research questions and methods have been premised on a positive perspective on female adolescent sexuality (Fine, 1988; Hurtado, 2003; Holland, Ramazanoglu, Sharpe, & Thomson, 2004; Thompson, 1990, 1995; Tolman, 1994, 2002), short of an epidemiological study, we have found collectively that for most girls, sexuality is most often not positive and is always complicated by the negative meanings (and quite often real material and social consequences) of their sexuality. This outcome of the desire to know the positive posits ironic limits to the question itself: it may not be there to be found. Research to date suggests that the gendered constructions of sexuality are at the heart of this no-finding finding. Anyway one cuts "positive," at least thus far in this body of research, it crops up only sporadically, infrequent but extraordinary interstices that are portals to the positive. Given this barren landscape, what then does it mean to pursue a research program on positive female adolescent sexuality? While ameliorating an unrelenting negative perspective predicated on risk and its prevention is unquestionably a good idea, might the speedy swing to positive be highly problematic?

What an unfettered mainstream approach to positive sexuality development may unintentionally obscure are the concentric contexts, the societal stuff from which girls and the people in their lives, and we, make meaning of their sexuality and its development, and in which they experience these processes. As I will describe below, Adrienne Rich's conception of compulsory heterosexuality (1983) offers a comprehensive way to conceptualize these contexts that keeps central the ways in which female sexuality has been at the heart of women's oppression and suppression. I suggest some re-visioning of this theory by incorporating theories of gender, race, and class that have been developed since Rich's seminal work,

NEW DIRECTIONS FOR CHILD AND ADOLESCENT DEVELOPMENT • DOI: 10.1002/cad

which provides fuel and pressure for grilling the concept of positive sexuality development for young women. With this framework, we can delineate strategies for more complex and nuanced approaches to the development of female adolescent sexuality.

Compulsory Heterosexuality Revis(ion)ed: Genealogy and Geometry

Carole Vance (1984) explicated the doubled reality of female sexuality within patriarchal society, of both pleasure and danger, arguing that focusing on one dimension to the exclusion of the other was simplistic and inconsistent with the circumstances of women's lives. Holding the tension of this contradiction is a necessary discomfort of feminist theorizing about sexuality. While some third-wave feminists claim the arrival of a new era in which young women's sexuality is whatever each wants it to be (Baumgardner & Richards, 2004), this perspective fails to explain the continued punitive meanings associated with female adolescent sexuality. Witness the panic over the possibility that "disturbed" girls are providing boys oral sex. To laminate female sexuality, to pigeonhole it as either pure pleasure or relentless risk, especially in adolescence, threatens to obscure the ongoing reality that societies (including much of our own) continue to be organized by and to maintain systemic male power in ever mutating guises (Levy, 2005; Fine, 2005). Perhaps unintentionally, it also implies a monolithic female sexuality that does not account for profound historical social inequalities that have and continue to implicate regulation of diverse women's sexuality as forms of control and oppression (Foucault, 1978; Lorde, 1984) into the twenty-first century (Collins, 2004; Harris, 2005; Hurtado & Sinha, 2005, Tolman, Madanagu, & Ozawa, 2005).

Rich's Theory of Compulsory Heterosexuality. In its original form and purpose, compulsory heterosexuality was theorized by Rich to expose the "erasure of lesbian existence" (1983, p. 185). While feminists of the late 1970s assumed that heterosexuality was natural and normal, Rich's starting point challenged (and revealed) this assumption. She asserted that instead, heterosexuality is produced through sets of belief and practice that both keep women apart and force women, both overtly and covertly, into partnerships with men. She argued that the reproduction of systemic male power and patriarchy is the political institution by which patriarchal society is reproduced and regulated. I will sidestep the contentious territory of her assertions regarding women's "natural" sexuality; what I am drawing attention to is the significance in her naming heterosexuality as a political institution.

She explicated how seamlessly woven together social processes that operate at the level of the individual, through personal relationships, culture, and the state, serve to produce and normalize heterosexuality. Compulsory heterosexuality works and retains its power because it is invisible as a political institution (Foucault, 1971). She made it visible. Much more than an individual's sexual orientation, Rich enabled us to see heterosexuality as a system that regulates women's sexuality by making visible and viable only one specific form of romantic and sexual relationship, thereby rendering it natural, normal, moral, and desirable.

Rich's position was that heterosexuality is compulsory for women, not only in being required but also in being actively pressed on women and girls, beginning at puberty. The evidence for her position, she maintained, is the "pervasive cluster of [physical, material, social and psychological] forces ranging from physical brutality to control of consciousness" (1983, p. 183) that seem necessary to maintain it, to make it at once desirable to and also punishable not to engage in heterosexual relationships (see Figure 6.1). While depressingly little of Rich's analysis remains unchanged, some dimensions have shifted and changed in relation to historically and culturally specific events (see Figure 6.2 for reconfigurations), illuminating the socially constructed dimensions of compulsory heterosexuality.

For instance, she names pornography as one such force. In her discussion of the negative impact of pornography on women, she articulates how it advertises women as sexual objects or sexual commodities to be consumed by males. Pornography shows women to be the natural sexual prey to men and that women love it; it also reinforces notions of both male and female sexual appetite as devoid of emotional context. Pornography portrays sexuality and violence as congruent. Rich's position was that pornography does

Figure 6.1. Rich's Compulsory Heterosexuality: A Map

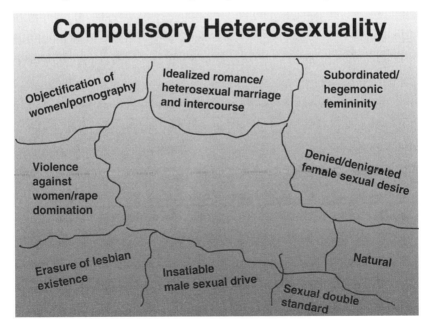

not simply create a climate in which sex and violence are interchangeable. Rather, it widens the range of behavior considered acceptable, even normal, from men in heterosexual intercourse, thus stripping women of autonomy, dignity, and sexual potential, including loving and being loved by women.

Hegemonic Femininity: Part of the Picture. Various feminist scholars have explicated another dimension of compulsory heterosexuality that is peppered throughout, though not named specifically in, Rich's original essay. Expectations of how women and girls should and should not feel, behave, and think regarding themselves, their own bodies, their roles in relationships, and their responses to expectations about men and boys can be conceptualized collectively as *hegemonic femininity* (included in Figure 6.1). This term means that only one specific form of femininity is made to seem legitimate, natural, and normal (Brown & Gilligan, 1992; Collins, 1990; Tolman & Porche, 2000). Sandra Bartky (1990) has written about how women, in order to feel appropriate and normal, are under pressure to embody specific behaviors and appearance that constitute this dominant form of femininity. These norms include particular forms of comportment and body management and containment that, she argues, produce the physical and psychological constraints evident among (White, middle-class) girls and women. Frederickson and Roberts (1997) have articulated and tested what they call self-objectification theory, whereby girls over the course of adolescence (and more recently later childhood) learn how to make themselves into sexual objects not only for the consumption of others but also in their own eyes, that is, through an internalized male gaze.

Feminist developmental psychologists have traced how women learn in adolescence to suppress "unladylike" emotions, including anger, learn to be "nice and kind," and avoid conflict to preserve relationships (Brown & Gilligan, 1992; Jordan, Surrey, Kaplan, Miller, & Stiver, 1991, Miller, 1976). Jane Ussher (1991) uses Butler's concept of gender performance to articulate how young women "manage" the demands of hegemonic femininity, through enacting different approaches to it: "being," "doing," "rejecting," or "subverting." Hegemonic femininity demands that (good) girls not have sexual agency, that is, a sense of themselves as sexual beings entitled to feel and act on their own feelings (Fine, 1988; Tolman, 1994, 2002).

Another Body of Knowledge: Hegemonic Masculinity. There are surprisingly few references to men in Rich's presentation of compulsory heterosexuality; one of the few explicit mentions is that women learn that male sexual desire is a right. A number of scholars have been studying what they denote *hegemonic masculinity* in the development and lives of men as a mirror to how Rich described compulsory heterosexuality restricting women. Hegemonic masculinity is the dominant conception of manhood, encompassing a set of norms and behaviors that men must strive to demonstrate—to themselves and to others—that they are "real men" (remember *Real Men Don't Eat Quiche?*). These norms demand that men deny most emotions, save for anger; be hard at all times and in all ways; engage in objectification of women and sex itself; and participate in the continuum of violence against women.

NEW DIRECTIONS FOR CHILD AND ADOLESCENT DEVELOPMENT • DOI: 10.1002/cad

The hegemony of this form of masculinity makes it seem to be the natural and normal way to demonstrate one's masculinity even while it diminishes men's humanity. It holds out false or impoverished possibilities of access to systemic male power for large numbers of men (Connell, 1987; Kimmel, 2000). Connell (1987) claimed that the most important feature of hegemonic masculinity is that it is heterosexual, by which he means connected to the institution of marriage. He theorized that there are multiple forms of masculinity but that these forms are differentially subordinated to hegemonic masculinity. He identified homosexuality as a subordinated masculinity. He also argues for emphasized rather than hegemonic femininity, in that femininity is also always subordinated to hegemonic masculinity. However, if looking from women's perspective, as is the standpoint of Rich's theory, a hegemonic form of femininity looms large.

Revis(ion)ing Compulsory Heterosexuality. In scanning Rich's description of compulsory heterosexuality, it is no surprise that there is little about men, save the ways in which constructions of men and operationalizations of male power oppress women. Rich's project was about illuminating how (and asking why) compulsory heterosexuality accomplishes the outcome of making lesbian desire, lesbian relationships, and lesbian community invisible (see also Pharr, 1988). Her project is to illuminate how the institution of heterosexuality is compulsory for women and the mechanisms by which women are compelled. However, if one considers the institution of heterosexuality from a heterosexual perspective and also from a developmental perspective, the proverbial "it takes two to tango" emerges: boys and men, too, are engaged in the process of reproducing heterosexuality, and it is compulsory for men as well. I chose her articulation of pornography to make a point about her theory: it demands to know how men's engagement with compulsory heterosexuality is necessary for it to work.

Scholars of masculinity have been concerned primarily with men's lives and struggles within the complexity of hegemonic masculinity and its relation to subordinated other forms of masculinities, suggesting that these masculinities be examined in conjunction with compulsory heterosexuality. This formulation of the relationship between masculinity and compulsory heterosexuality may also be an artifact of Rich's noninclusion of male homosexuality into her theory. Masculinity scholars have argued for the potent interplay between hegemonic masculinity and homophobia (against men specifically), in that homophobia functions to produce and sustain hegemonic masculinity by patrolling its borders and punishing or threatening those who cross (Epstein, 1996) or open them. In popular parlance, hegemonic masculinity is codependent with homophobia.

My revis(ion)ing of Rich's theory rests on the introjection of hegemonic masculinity twinned with homophobia against men into the very center of compulsory heterosexuality (see Figure 6.2). Why does hegemonic masculinity occupy the center of Figure 6.2? I suggest that hegemonic masculinity, profoundly joined with homophobia, has a strong role to play for girls as well as for boys in the reproduction of heterosexuality, as an institution and also as a set of practices, at the individual, relational, and institutional and cultural levels. These two potent and reinforcing forces fuel the systemic maintenance of male power through their power and salience for both boys and girls. I suggest that hegemonic femininity is complementary to hegemonic masculinity even as the latter lays claim to and promise of relatively more power. The qualities that constitute hegemonic femininity incite (that is, motivate without being evident as doing so) internal and external regulation of women's bodies, minds, hearts, and powers; as described above, what characterizes and mobilizes masculinity is more than anything that which is not feminine (Kimmel, 1996).

Dialectic Between Theory and Research. Shifting the paradigm of compulsory heterosexuality to include rather than only indict boys and men provides a new framework for the development of gendered sexualities. One such framework includes understanding how the interplay between various forces and institutions press on boys and men and on girls and women to (re)produce compulsory heterosexuality. Some outlines of this interplay have become evident in research on young women's and young men's sexuality that is grounded in their perspectives and voices or discourses (Fine, 1992; Gilligan, 1982; Hollway, 1989). In their qualitative study of girls' and boys' choices about safer sex and negotiation within heterosexual relationships, Holland et al. (2004) found what they call "the male in the head" as

Figure 6.2. Compulsory Heterosexuality Revis(ion)ed

Compulsory Heterosexuality Revis(ion)ed

Objectification of women/pornography

Idealized romance/ heterosexual marriage and intercourse

Subordinated/ hegemonic Femininity

Homophobia

Violence against women/rape Domination constant threat

Denial/denigrated female sexual desire

Hegemonic Masculinity

Persecution/resistance to queer existence

Insatiable male sexual drive

Natural

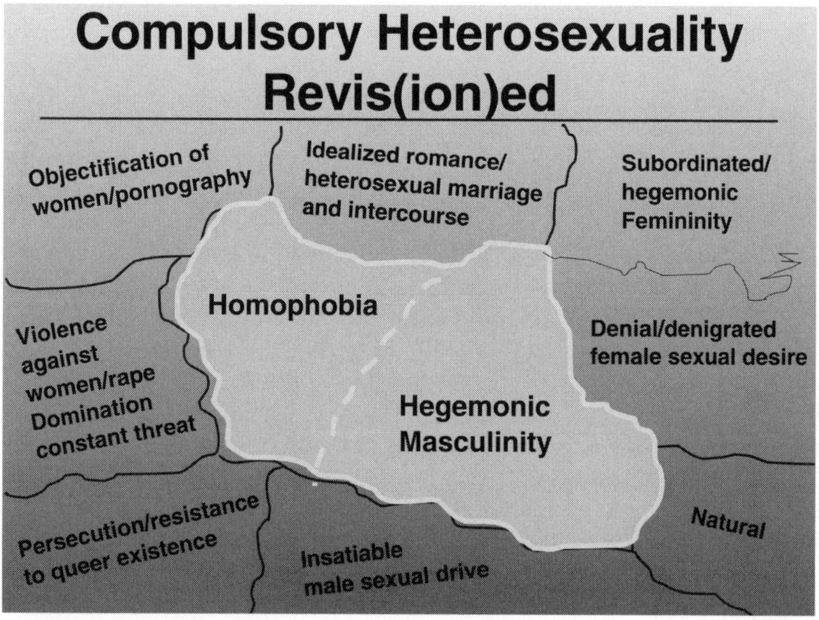

a profound force for both boys and girls. In fact, they report that they found no evidence of female sexual subjectivity.

In beginning to study how early adolescent males narrate their experiences with sexuality and relationships, my group began to hear two things. One is partially what the masculinity theorists have outlined regarding systematic male dominance over women. At the cusp of adolescence, boys describe the importance of demonstrating to their male friends, and less importantly to girls, that they can control and coerce girls, that they want to "get sex" all the time, and that they demonstrate their heterosexuality publicly, thereby making visible that they are not homosexual (Tolman, Spencer, Porche & Rosen-Reynoso, 2003). Some boys also describe the tension between their desire to have authentic relationships with girls, to be close, to be curious sexually but not especially interested in sexual conquest.

The second thing is how boys' or males' developing engagement with adult masculinity bears on girls' negotiation of romantic or heterosexual interactions and relationships, balancing the desire for romance with their perceptions of the need to protect themselves from boys as they engage in enactments of masculinity, which can be accomplished by engaging in the practice of hegemonic femininity. Listening to adolescent boys and girls in tandem, we heard them narrating how compulsory heterosexuality becomes an organizing principle in their developing sexuality at the early stages of their experiences with sexuality in adolescence. In an entirely different project, Holland et al. (2004) identified a similar process in how older teenage and young adult women and men negotiate and think about their own safety in the context of practicing safer sex, in particular noting a lack of a sense of entitlement that women's descriptions reflected to their own needs and even safety.

This research illuminates that central to the reproduction of compulsory heterosexuality is the complementary and systematic "call and response" or repartee that exists with hegemonic masculinity and hegemonic femininity for both girls/women and boys/men. Rather than being opposites, these gender constructs fit together, complementing one another, as two cogs in the machine of compulsory heterosexuality. Just as this research forms a dialectic with theories of femininity and masculinity, thus transforming compulsory heterosexuality, this process also offers a compelling alternative for how to keep gender central and salient in the study of positive female adolescent sexuality.

Gender Complementarity as an Analytical Principle: The Prequel. The history of evaluating sex differences in social and developmental psychology is a long one, and arguments about whether there really are differences continue to rage. The prevailing approach in developmental psychology for investigating gender differences is to evaluate whether girls/women and men/boys are different or the same or similar (Hyde, 2005). In part, this approach may reflect the embeddedness of dualistic thinking in society and culture, an entrenched evolutionary viewpoint, and resistance to theorizing power as a central dynamic in development. The focus on gender differences is also reflective of the preferred methodologies of psychology, that is, statistical analyses can identify and make meaning of differences but almost always (with the exception of population-based studies and meta-analyses) cannot interpret failure to find differences.

Compulsory heterosexuality, revis(ion)ed, challenges and rebuffs the question of difference as inadequate. I propose the use of *gender complementarity* as a principle for incorporating gender in a new way into the emerging study of positive adolescent sexuality development. Use of this analytical principle reflects different assumptions about gender and how girls/women and boys/men are positioned in relation to one another, so that rather than asking whether a particular outcome is the same or different for boys and girls, one identifies different outcomes that are salient to each gender and reflect gender complementarity in lieu of gender differences.

Gender complementarity calls for investigation of how the aspects of behavior, experiences, emotional lives, and expectations that are differentially meaningful to girls and boys dovetail to reproduce compulsory heterosexuality. That is, rather than identifying a neutral outcome, such as how frequently adolescents have protected sexual intercourse and then investigating whether there are gender differences in the relative rates, we can identify what is not neutral about the outcome. Thus, the gendered meaning of the behavior of performing or receiving oral sex would have to be at the center of the research question, design, analysis, and interpretation, considering the gender complementarity of this kind of heterosexual interaction. Before offering more specific examples, though, a final revis(ion)ing of compulsory heterosexuality is necessary.

Infusing Race, Ethnicity, and Class in Revis(ion)ing Compulsory Heterosexuality. There is one final revision required in this new mapping: incorporating race, class, and ethnicity into the theory itself. While the point of hegemonic masculinity is to make it seem as if there is only one way to be masculine, there are many practiced masculinities (Connell, 1987), subversive as well as subverted; the same is true for femininities (Brown, 1998; Fordham, 1988). Kimberle Crenshaw's theory of intersectionality, whereby gender, race, and class interplay to generate positionalities in social landscapes (1992), is essential in revis(ion)ing compulsory heterosexuality once more to reflect and illuminate this multiplicity in how compulsory heterosexuality operates for various communities. That is, identifying various interplaying femininities and masculinities, and how they are constructed in relation to hegemonic masculinity and hegemonic femininity, is a critical part of acknowledging and investigating how compulsory heterosexuality as an institution holds race and class hierarchies as a constituent dimension.

Patricia Hill Collins (2004) observed that hegemonic masculinity "is fundamentally a dynamic, relational construct . . . that is shaped by ideologies of gender, age, class, sexuality and race. . . . Without these groups as markers, hegemonic masculinity becomes meaningless" (p. 185). Rich's theory did not account for these systemic hierarchies, as has been noted by

Black lesbian feminists (Lorde, 1984), Latina scholars (Hurtado, 1996), and feminist scholars of Black femininities and masculinities (Collins, 2004). While Connell (1987) explicated how working-class masculinities operate in relation to hegemonic masculinity, the missing discourse of race may explain his positing femininity as emphasized rather than hegemonic. This stance disregards hierarchical relationships between White middle-class and wealthy women and White poor women, or between middle-class Black women and poor Latinas, or the well-documented racialized femininities that impact women's relationships with each other and with men.

Collins (2004) has explicated the gender complementarity of Black femininities and Black masculinities as formulated and also cannibalized as practices for the hegemonic forms. She analyzes how class is a profoundly complicating factor in evaluating how these gender hegemonies work together. While hegemonic forms are always part of the picture, there can be other dominant femininities and masculinities within communities that regulate community members, as well as often demeaning or dehumanizing forms that assert systematic and systemic (White, middle-class) male power and, in some conditions, the relative power of specific groups of women. While incorporating heterosexism into the constellation of structural inequalities she explicates, Collins does not reference compulsory heterosexuality in her discussion of gender complementarity.

Currently, I am struggling to map how compulsory heterosexuality intersects with or is present in some relation to forms that are more local, in this case focusing on the significant social systems that underpin interactions in the United States: race, ethnicity, and class. In addition, these multiple mappings of compulsory heterosexuality are always in motion even as they seem fixed; that is, they shift in meaning, form, and practice through time and space. At this point in time, I envision mapping this fuller conceptualization as essentially three-dimensional (or multidimensional) and thus impossible to picture in this two-dimensional space. A third figure, then, must be constructed in the reader's imagination. Imagine the map in Figure 6.2 turned horizontally in space, and then envision it hovering over two, three, or multiple other maps—one mapping compulsory heterosexuality as it exists in African American communities, incorporating hegemonic Black masculinity and hegemonic Black femininity, another Latino, another working-class White—that are constantly aligning and colliding. I am sure that the position of these subordinated maps would be subject to a jarring jostling, to portray the dynamic relations to one another. They might even tip or rip the dominant map in places, especially over time.

The Analytical Principle of Gender Complementarity: Fully Loaded. With the disruption of the monolithic girl/boy but retention of hegemonic masculinity and femininity, the application of gender complementarity as an analytical principle can be explored. A positive question might be: How do (Black, Latina, middle-class) girls negotiate being labeled "slut," and what are their responses to (any) negative consequences? For

NEW DIRECTIONS FOR CHILD AND ADOLESCENT DEVELOPMENT • DOI: 10.1002/cad

boys, the question is necessarily different: Do (Asian American, working-class, Chinese) boys feel compelled to engage in sexual behavior, and if so, how do they respond?

Asking the complementary and layered questions of diverse boys is salient to research on diverse girls' sexuality development because of how both are situated within compulsory heterosexuality (Figure 6.2 and the imagined third figure). Any potential positive sexuality development involves some form of resistance to hegemonic femininity and hegemonic masculinity (and other dominant cultural femininities and masculinities) and then also other dimensions of compulsory heterosexuality. By destabilizing gender differences through complicating gendered interactions, gender complementarity as a principle in designing, conducting, and analyzing research means identifying different but complementary outcomes, constructs, phenomena, and experiences to study for girls (and for boys). Buoyed by the gravitas of theory, revis(ion)ed compulsory heterosexuality becomes more than a context for development. It can be integrated or blended with a specific developmental theory to account for a mechanism of development. In my own work, I use relational theory (Gilligan, 1982; Jordan et al., 1991), which incorporates psychodynamic processes such as internalization, denial, and resistance. That is, compulsory heterosexuality itself is necessary but not sufficient in the study of positive adolescent female sexuality development.

Gaining Ground by Mixing Methods

I hope that this revision can be particularly helpful for developing a complex research agenda dedicated to seeking positive female adolescent sexuality. Revi(sion)ed compulsory heterosexuality provides strong support for the need to understand what is perhaps most salient for girls' positive sexuality development: What gets in the way? What does resistance to compulsory heterosexuality look like, sound like, incorporate, require, cost? While acknowledging that young people are developing sexuality and have a right to do so in healthy ways (Satcher, 2001), efforts to chart positive female sexuality development require accounting for gendered constructions and consequences of sexuality within compulsory heterosexuality (Tolman et al., 2003).

Such a shift would demand the use of a range of methodologies, since it is premised in part on understanding the meanings of behaviors and experiences. For instance, to pursue a positive female sexuality developmental question could mean the study of what specifically gets in the way of positive sexuality for various groups of girls depending on their relation to compulsory heterosexuality in its hegemonic and more local forms. Mobilizing multiple methods can flesh out the contradictions, nuances, and individual "takes" across and within group patterns. Kincheloe's elaboration of Denzin and Lincoln's concept of bricolage—"the process of getting down to the nuts and bolts of multidisciplinary research" (2005,

p. 323)—is useful for considering how to operationalize this revis(ion)ed theory of compulsory heterosexuality. This theoretical framework enables and insists on "focusing on webs of relationships instead of simply things-in-themselves . . . construct[ing] the object of study in a more complex framework . . . direct[ing] attention toward processes, relationships, and interconnections among phenomena" (p. 323) and, for the purposes of developmental questions, the ways in which individuals develop and know themselves through being always situated in such webs.

For instance, in my own work, I have posed and answered questions that require both qualitative and quantitative methods (Tolman & Szalacha, 1999) to determine whether and to what extent hegemonic masculinity and femininity explain the gender-salient outcomes of endorsement of coercion in heterosexual relationships among White working-class and middle-class early adolescent boys and among poor and working-class Latinos and beliefs in romance conventions among comparable groups of girls. The finding that masculinity ideology is the strongest predictor of endorsement of both coercion for boys and romance conventions for girls (with an interaction for Latinas but not Latinos) suggests an important new direction for understanding positive sexuality development among girls. The dovetailing qualitative component of this study illuminates through thematic analysis of narratives about sexuality and gender within heterosexual relationships what compliance, questioning, and resistant engagement with compulsory heterosexuality sound like for these girls and boys, giving voice to the complementary quality of this variability (Tolman, 2004).

In a Different Position: Forging New Directions

In an essay entitled "Lusting for Freedom," Rebecca Walker (2001) describes her experience of sexuality development in adolescence:

> [I knew that] I deserved to live free of shame, that my body is not my enemy and that pleasure is my friend and my right. Without this core . . . how else would I have learned to follow and cultivate my own desire? How else would I have learned to listen to and develop the language of my own body? How else would I have learned to initiate, sustain and develop healthy intimacy. . . . The question is not whether young women are going to have sex, for this is far beyond any parental or societal control. The question is rather, what do young women need to make sex a dynamic, affirming, safe and pleasurable part of our lives [pp. 22–23]?

In *Dilemmas of Desire* (2002), I found that for virtually all—but not all—of the girls with whom I spoke from both urban and suburban public schools, their own sexuality was a dilemma for them. While they could identify the double standard, they did not understand why it existed and offered the naturalized explanation: that's the way things are. Such depopulated sentences perpetuate and reproduce the cover story for girls' desire and its systematic denial. The girls who were notable exceptions described entitlement to their own sexual desire and agency, resonating with Walker's words. Three-quarters of the several hundred girls interviewed by Sharon Thompson (1990, 1995) described their first experiences of (hetero)sexual intercourse as painful, disappointing, and boring. Unlike the remaining "pleasure narrators," whose mothers had conveyed to them a sense of entitlement to pleasure and safety, a positive position on their sexuality, they had no expectation that it should be a positive experience. Walker paints a glorious picture of positive female adolescent development. How can such differences be explained? The revis(ion)ed form of compulsory heterosexuality holds these extremely different experiences of female sexuality for young women. Resistance to conventional romance and hegemonic femininity, as well as to hegemonic masculinity and various beliefs about adolescent and male sexuality, not only offers explanation but also alternative stories by which to live as girls, mothers, educators, and policymakers.

As Judith Butler has articulated, "Fantasy is what establishes the possible in excess of the real; it points, it points elsewhere, and when it is embodied, it brings the elsewhere home" (2004, p. 217). Sandra Bem (1995) suggested that rather than trying to diminish sex differences, as she did in her early work, which, she concluded, covers up compulsory heterosexuality, a more productive route would be to "turn up the volume" on it. She urges psychologists to understand how compulsory heterosexuality is reproduced through specified, condoned, narrow, and limiting and limited gender conventions by acknowledging why gender compliance must be compulsively repeated. Butler suggests that revealing forms of gender and sexuality that elude and refute compulsory heterosexuality through strategies and performances of revelatory and revolutionary genders and sexualities can and will destabilize what she calls the heterosexual matrix (similar to compulsory heterosexuality in less specified form).

The search to describe and trace positive female adolescent sexuality can take advantage of this revision of Rich's theory to make visible both the framework and fissures that are the lived experiences of developing adolescent girls to illuminate how it works and also alternatives that will inevitably destabilize it. For instance, Lisa Diamond's work on young women's rejection of specific categories of sexual identities (2000) and the growing visibility of intersex and transgendered people are revealing (or perhaps dismantling) compulsory heterosexuality. These public displays of nonconformity illuminate how it underpins our social structures and psychological schemas and how exploding categories makes space for positive female sexuality and its development, albeit discomfiting for many.

Speaking Powerfully to Power. At the same time, it is crucial to take the larger context of girls' lives into account, especially with the growth of a global commercialization of desire (Harris, 2005). While positive sexuality may gain space to develop, we must keep vigilant about what Michelle Fine calls the "contemporary perversions [that have resulted from feminist

New Directions for Child and Adolescent Development • DOI: 10.1002/cad

calls for girls' sexual freedom]: the commodification of [girls'] desire and the appropriation of 'protection' as the embodiment of danger" (2005, p. 57). What is positive sexuality development for young women who are fighting for their education to extricate themselves from lives of poverty, for whom desire is "gravy" (Burns & Torre, 2005, p. 22)?

As positive sexuality development emerges as a significant line of study in developmental psychology, it is crucial that we wrest the discourse and lay claim to what constitutes positive sexuality for girls. What is positive for one constituency (say, feminist psychologists) is likely not for another (say, those who are trying to maintain compulsory heterosexuality through policy and laws about marriage). We need to think strategically about engaging with the prevailing discourse in order to interrupt it. We can "prove" what positive sexuality is for girls by conducting studies that associate positive dimensions of their sexuality development with other positive outcomes (Impett, Schooler, & Tolman, in press). Another strategy would be to use other developmental research to guide and legitimate this endeavor. For instance, we could capitalize on Jean Rhodes's compelling research on how mentoring works (2002) and evaluate the differences between matched groups of girls who have "sexual mentors" and those who do not. I even asked a researcher who studies female sexual desire in rats if he thought that rats had a patriarchal society. He took this question seriously and remarked that although he thought not, shifting hormonal conditions could possibly affect gendered sexual interactions (J. Pfaus, personal communication, January 2003).

At a time when chastity rings costing three hundred dollars appear as the "latest item" on the Style page of the *New York Times* (Rosenbloom, 2005), when it is anathema even to suggest that girls see sex therapists, although they describe their sexuality in ways that would, in adult women, merit treatment by (or plastering over with) the latest medications, we need to ask how (all forms of) sex education treat, cover up, or reify hegemonic and other masculinities and femininities. The more that we explore and document how gendered conceptions of sexuality and hegemonic constructions of gender operate in the real lives of girls (and boys) as they develop, the more we can deploy research as a tool of resistance to the ways that compulsory heterosexuality makes girls (and boys) vulnerable to unhealthy relationships, threatening their ability to explore sexuality.

The good news is that sexual development is morphing into sexuality development. The process of girls' bodies changing into women's is an absolutely central anchor of female sexuality development, not only for girls' experiencing new feelings, experimenting with new forms of embodiment, and playing malleable identities, but also for how they start to be processed and treated as the sexual beings they are becoming. We can now aspire to mapping multiple trajectories of sexuality development for girls and for boys within and, on occasion, against compulsory heterosexuality. By incorporating gender complementarity intersecting with race, ethnicity, and class in various parts of the country and in different cultural communities and social circumstances, we can acknowledge from the start that no universal trajectory should be expected. This stance would enable us to tussle with the very idea of what constitutes positive sexuality and its development. Engagement with this question will undoubtedly mean weaving together the vibrant, potentially garish, and clashing colors of real-life contexts. Such fabrics will range from enabling the decoupling of girls' sexuality from their reproductive capacity through effective contraceptive options that are not universally available (and are even on the cultural chopping block now) to how sexuality can invite new vulnerabilities to sexually transmitted infections and HIV. Thus far in my own work, I have focused on heterosexual girls by fiat (school-based samples), but I believe the revis(ion)ed theory of compulsory heterosexuality can be useful in considering the experiences of lesbian, bisexual, and queer girls (and also boys), who do not identify with a specific sexual orientation, and especially exciting for research on transgendered adolescents.

Finally, we need to ask the taboo questions that are taboo because they may reveal positive adolescent girls' sexuality development and exercise our entire arsenal of methods (biomarkers, ethnographies, behavioral diaries, phenomenological interviews, developing new measures). If one considers the end point of adolescent sexuality development to include the incorporation of the pleasures of sexuality—physical, emotional, relational—along with awareness of the vulnerabilities of sexuality into one's sexual self-concept—then we include pleasure, passion, mutuality, safety, embodiment, agency, experiencing emotions, and vulnerability as developmentally expected for both girls and boys, expanding in tandem (perhaps with deepening intimacy) through adolescence. From a positive point of view, we might ask girls when they first had sexual feelings and orgasms, and what these were like. How did they make sense of them? How did they respond? What is different about sexual experiences out of relationships versus within relationships for girls who differ in myriad ways? How does this change at different points in their development? If lesbian and bisexual girls are challenging labels, what might inspire heterosexual girls to do so? There are numerous questions that we as adults will never think to ask, and so creating alliances with youth as standard practice will explicate salient questions and issues. We could refuse the limiting of knowledge that comes from keeping it within the ivory tower. We should insist that "applied" developmental research is a misnomer. We can broaden our theoretical palettes.

Optimism from a Skeptic. The chances that the knowledge that can come from inquiries and research agendas might have an impact on public policy are heartening; the discipline of developmental psychology does hold authority to say what is "normal" and "normative," and even "positive," and deploys it whenever reputable volumes like this one are published. The opportunity to change psychological and public discourses about girls' and adolescent sexuality, to be able to conduct such research with funding, to ask such questions without having one's legitimacy (and sanity and moral character) questioned and employment prospects and security endangered, is tantalizing. Those of us who brought adolescence to feminist theory and research on female sexuality (most important being Sharon Thompson), and feminist theory and research methods for studying female sexuality to adolescence (initiated by Michelle Fine), were working in a moment of possibility. This exciting endeavor is underway, as is evident in the burgeoning of new research questions, interview protocols, and measures that bring into focus concepts like sexual assertiveness, sexual agency, and sexual arousal as positive qualities that we should expect girls to develop (O'Sullivan, 2005; Horne & Zimmer-Gembeck, 2005). We can and should make less tentative forays into the unknown worlds of girls' pleasure, power, ecstasy, arousal, fantasies, and desires that refuse to be boxed in by categories. To do so with integrity, respect, and an unimpeachable desire to know, we need to face the continued complexity that positive female adolescent sexuality strikes at the very heart of compulsory heterosexuality. Rather than avoid the crisis by backing off, we can dispel it by pushing forward, refusing to simplify the contradictory realities of female sexuality development in an enragingly familiar patriarchal world.

References

Bartky, S. (1990). *Femininity and domination*. New York: Routledge.

Baumgardner, J., & Richards, A. (2004). Feminism and femininity: Or how we learned to stop worrying and love the thong. In A. Harris (Ed.), *All about the girl: Culture, power and identity*. New York: Routledge.

Bem, S. (1995). Dismantling gender polarization and compulsory heterosexuality: Should we turn the volume down or up? *Journal of Sex Research, 32*, 329–334.

Brown, L. M. (1998). *Raising their voices: The politics of girls' anger*. Cambridge, MA: Harvard University Press.

Brown, L. M., & Gilligan, C. (1992). *Meeting at the crossroads: Women's psychology and girls' development*. Cambridge, MA: Harvard University Press.

Burns, A., & Torre, M. (2005). Revolutionary sexualities. *Feminism and Psychology, 15*(1), pp. 21–26.

Butler, J. (1990). *Gender trouble: Feminism and the subversion of identity*. New York: Routledge.

Butler, J. (2004). *Undoing gender*. New York: Routledge.

Collins, P. H. (1990). *Black feminist thought: Knowledge, consciousness and the politics of consciousness*. Boston: Unwin Hyman.

Collins, P. H. (2004). *Black sexual politics: African-Americans, gender and the new racism*. New York: Routledge.

Connell, R. (1987). *Gender and power*. Palo Alto, CA: Stanford University Press.

Crenshaw, K. (1992/1996). Mapping the margins: Intersectionality, identity politics and violence against women of color. In K. Crenshaw, (ed.). Critical race theory: The key writings that formed the movement. New York, NY: New Press, 357-383.

Diamond, L. (2000). Sexual identity, attractions and behavior among young sexual-minority women over a two-year period. *Developmental Psychology, 36*(2), 241–250.

Epstein, D. (1996). Border patrols: Policing the boundaries of heterosexuality. In British Sociological Society (Ed.), *Sex, sensibility and the gendered body*. New York: St. Martin's Press.

NEW DIRECTIONS FOR CHILD AND ADOLESCENT DEVELOPMENT • DOI: 10.1002/cad

Fine, M. (1988). Female adolescents, sexuality, and schooling: The missing discourse of desire. *Harvard Educational Review, 58*(1), 29–53.

Fine, M. (1992). *Disruptive voices: The possibilities of feminist research.* Ann Arbor: University of Michigan Press.

Fine, M. (2005). Desire: The morning (and fifteen years) after. *Feminism and Psychology, 15*(1), 54–60.

Fordham, S. (1988). Those loud Black girls: Pyrrhic victory. *Harvard Educational Review, 58*(1), 54–62.

Foucault, M. (1978). *The history of sexuality.* New York: Vintage Books.

Frederickson, B. L., & Roberts, T. A. (1997). Objectification theory: Toward understanding women's lived experiences and mental health risks. *Psychology of Women Quarterly, 21,* 173–206.

Gilligan, C. (1982). *In a different voice.* Cambridge, MA: Harvard University Press.

Harris, A. (2005). Discourses of desire as governmentality: Young women, sexuality and the significance of safe spaces. *Feminism and Psychology, 15*(1), 39–43.

Holland, J., Ramazanoglu, C., Sharpe, S., & Thomson, R. (2004). *The male in the head: Young people, heterosexuality and power.* London: Falmer Press.

Hollway, W. (1989). *Subjectivity and method in psychology: Gender, meaning and science.* Thousand Oaks, CA: Sage.

Horne, S., & Zimmer-Gembeck, M. (2005). Female subjectivity and well-being: Comparing late adolescents with different sexual experiences. *Sexuality Research and Social Policy, 2*(3), 25–40.

Hurtado, A. (1996). *The color of privilege: Three blasphemies on race and feminism.* Ann Arbor: University of Michigan Press.

Hurtado, A. (2003). *Voicing Chicana feminisms: Young women speak out on sexuality and identity.* New York: NYU Press.

Hurtado, A., & Sinha, M. (2005). Restriction and freedom in the construction of sexuality: Young Chicanas and Chicanos speak out. *Feminism and Psychology, 15*(1), 33–38.

Hyde, J. (2005). The gender similarities hypothesis. *American Psychologist, 60*(6), 581–592.

Impett, E., Schooler, D., & Tolman, D. (in press). Femininity ideology and female adolescents' sexual health. *Archives of Sexual Behavior.*

Jordan, J., Surrey, J., Kaplan, A., Miller, J., & Stiver, I. (1991). *Women's growth in connections: Writings from the Stone Center.* New York: Guilford Press.

Kimmel, M. (1996). *Manhood in America: A cultural history.* New York: Free Press.

Kimmel, M. (2000). *The gendered society.* New York: Oxford University Press.

Kincheloe, J. (2005). On to the next level: Continuing the conceptualization of the bricolage. *Qualitative Inquiry, 11*(3), 323–350.

Levy, A. (2005). *Female chauvinist pigs: Women and the rise of raunch culture.* New York: Free Press.

Lorde, A. (1984). *Sister Outsider: Essays and speeches.* Freedom, CA: Crossing Press.

Miller, J. (1976). *Towards a new psychology of women.* Boston: Beacon Press.

O'Sullivan, L. (2005). The social and relationship contexts and cognitions associated with romantic and sexual experiences of early-adolescent girls. *Sexuality Research and Social Policy, 2*(3), 13–24.

Pharr, S. (1988/1997). *Homophobia: A weapon of sexism.* San Francisco, CA: Chardon Press.

Rich, A. (1983). Compulsory heterosexuality and lesbian existence. In A. Snitow, C. Stansell, & S. Thompson (Eds.), *The power of desire* (pp. 177–205). New York: Monthly Review Press.

Rhodes, J. (2002). *Stand by me.* Cambridge, MA: Harvard University Press.

Rosenbloom, S. (2005, December 8). A ring that says no, not yet. *New York Times,* Thursday Style Section, 5A.

NEW DIRECTIONS FOR CHILD AND ADOLESCENT DEVELOPMENT • DOI: 10.1002/cad

Rubin, G. (1984). Thinking sex: Notes for a radical theory of the politics of sexuality. In C. Vance (Ed.), *Pleasure and danger: Exploring female sexuality*. New York: Routledge.

Russell, S. (2005). Introduction to positive perspectives on adolescent sexuality: Part 1. *Sexuality Research and Social Policy, 2*(3), 1–3.

Satcher, D. (2001). *The surgeon general's call to action to promote sexual health and responsible sexual behavior*. Washington, D.C.: U.S. Department of Health and Human Services.

Thompson, S. (1990). Putting a big thing in a little hole: Teenage girls' accounts of sexual initiation. *Journal of Sex Research, 27*(3), 341–361.

Thompson, S. (1995). *Going all the way: Teenage girls' tales of romance, sex and pregnancy*. New York: Hill and Wang.

Tolman, D. (1994). Doing desire: Adolescent girls' struggles for/with sexuality. *Gender and Society, 8*(3), 324–342.

Tolman, D. (2002). *Dilemmas of desire: Teenage girls talk about sexuality*. Cambridge, MA: Harvard University Press.

Tolman, D. (2004, October). *Not for girls only: Compulsory heterosexuality and adolescent sexuality*. Paper presented at the Society for the Scientific Study of Sexuality, Atlanta, GA.

Tolman, D., Madanagu, B., & Ozawa, G. (2005). Supporting subjectivity: Girls' power initiative as gender practice (a conversation). *Feminism and Psychology, 15*(1), 50–53.

Tolman, D. L., & Porche, M. V. (2000). The Adolescent Femininity Ideology Scale: Development and validation of a new measure for girls. *Psychology of Women Quarterly, 24*, 365–376.

Tolman, D., Spencer, R., Porche, M., & Rosen-Reynoso, M. (2003). Sowing the seeds of violence in heterosexual relationships: Early adolescents narrate compulsory heterosexuality. *Journal of Social Issues, 59*(1), 159–178.

Tolman, D., Striepe, M., & Harmon, T. (2003). Gender matters: Constructing (a) model(s) of adolescent sexual health. *Journal of Sex Research, 40*(1), 4–12.

Tolman, D., & Szalacha, L. (1999). Dimensions of desire: Bridging qualitative and quantitative methods in a study of female adolescent sexuality. *Psychology of Women Quarterly, 23*(2), 7–39.

Ussher, J. (1991). *Fantasies of femininity*. New York: Routledge.

Vance, C. (1984). Introduction. In C. Vance (Ed.), *Pleasure and danger: Exploring female sexuality*. New York: Routledge.

Walker, R. (2001). Lusting for freedom. In B. Findlan (Ed.), *Listen up: Voices from the next feminist generation*. Seattle, WA: Seal Press.

DEBORAH L. TOLMAN *is the director of the Center for Research on Gender and Sexuality and Professor of Human Sexuality Studies at San Francisco State University.*

NEW DIRECTIONS FOR CHILD AND ADOLESCENT DEVELOPMENT • DOI: 10.1002/cad

INDEX

Back Issue/Subscription Order Form

Copy or detach and send to:

Jossey-Bass, A Wiley Imprint, 989 Market Street, San Francisco CA 94103-1741
Call or fax toll-free: Phone 888-378-2537 6:30AM–3PM PST; Fax 888-481-2665

Back Issues: Please send me the following issues at $29 each

(Important: please indicate the New Directions title initials and issue numbers—for example, "CD99" for New Directions in Child and Adolescent Development, number 99.)

_____

_____

_____

$ _____ Total for single issues

$ _____ SHIPPING CHARGES: SURFACE   Domestic   Canadian
                               First Item $5.00 $6.00
                               Each Add'l Item $3.00 $1.50

For next-day and second-day delivery rates, call the number listed above.

Subscriptions   Please ___ start ___ renew my subscription to *New Directions for Child and Adolescent Development* for the year 2_____ at the following rate:

U.S.   ___ Individual $90   ___ Institutional $220
Canada   ___ Individual $90   ___ Institutional $260
All Others   ___ Individual $114   ___ Institutional $294

Online subscriptions are available via Wiley InterScience!

For more information about online subscriptions visit
www.wileyinterscience.com

$_____ Total single issues and subscriptions (Add appropriate sales tax for your state for single issue orders. No sales tax for U.S. subscriptions. Canadian residents, add GST for subscriptions and single issues.)

___ Payment enclosed (U.S. check or money order only)
___ VISA ___ MC ___ AmEx # _____ Exp. Date _____

Signature _____ Day Phone _____
___ Bill Me (U.S. institutional orders only. Purchase order required.)

Purchase order # _____

Federal Tax ID13559302   GST 89102 8052

Name _____

Address _____

_____

Phone _____ E-mail _____

For more information about Jossey-Bass, visit our Web site at www.josseybass.com

OTHER TITLES AVAILABLE IN THE
NEW DIRECTIONS FOR CHILD AND ADOLESCENT DEVELOPMENT SERIES
Reed W. Larson and Lene Arnett Jensen, Editors-in-Chief
William Damon, Founding Editor-in-Chief

NEW DIRECTIONS FOR CHILD AND ADOLESCENT DEVELOPMENT IS NOW AVAILABLE ONLINE AT WILEY INTERSCIENCE

What is Wiley InterScience?

Wiley InterScience is the dynamic online content service from John Wiley & Sons delivering the full text of over 300 leading scientific, technical, medical, and professional journals, plus major reference works, the acclaimed Current Protocols laboratory manuals, and even the full text of select Wiley print books online.

What are some special features of Wiley InterScience?

Wiley Interscience Alerts is a service that delivers table of contents via e-mail for any journal available on Wiley InterScience as soon as a new issue is published online.

EarlyView is Wiley's exclusive service presenting individual articles online as soon as they are ready, even before the release of the compiled print issue. These articles are complete, peer-reviewed, and citable.

CrossRef is the innovative multi-publisher reference linking system enabling readers to move seamlessly from a reference in a journal article to the cited publication, typically located on a different server and published by a different publisher.

How can I access Wiley InterScience?

Visit http://www.interscience.wiley.com.

Guest Users can browse Wiley InterScience for unrestricted access to journal tables of contents and article abstracts, or use the powerful search engine.

Registered Users are provided with a *Personal Home Page* to store and manage customized alerts, searches, and links to favorite journals and articles. Additionally, Registered Users can view free online sample issues and preview selected material from major reference works.

Licensed Customers are entitled to access full-text journal articles in PDF, with select journals also offering full-text HTML.

How do I become an Authorized User?

Authorized Users are individuals authorized by a paying Customer to have access to the journals in Wiley InterScience. For example, a university that subscribes to Wiley journals is considered to be the Customer. Faculty, staff and students authorized by the university to have access to those journals in Wiley InterScience are Authorized Users. Users should contact their library for information on which Wiley journals they have access to in Wiley InterScience.

ASK YOUR INSTITUTION ABOUT WILEY INTERSCIENCE TODAY!